MW00628392

# *Common* PLACE

# *Common* PLACE

## The Public Library, Civil Society, and Early American Values

*Thomas E. Johnson, Jr.*

*Levellers Press*
AMHERST, MASSACHUSETTS

Published by *Levellers Press*, Amherst, Massachusetts

Printed in the United States of America

ISBN 978-1-951928-57-5

*This book is dedicated to librarians in America—past, present, and future.*

# TABLE OF CONTENTS

# FOREWORD

My first experience in a public library was a visit to the Otis Library in Norwich, Connecticut when I was perhaps eight years old. I grew up the oldest of eight children in a home that had a collection of books started by my grandfather. My parents added books of interest to them. The children's books added to the collection were mostly gifts to us from aunts. The Otis Library's collection seemed vast to me and truly became an adventure in discovery. This early experience opened my eyes to what a community can do and be for its young people. I had found a treasure trove of books about history, science, places around the world, and stories of lives very different from my own. I took particular pleasure in working my way through the biography section. I first learned about Richard Nixon in 1962, long before he became president; read about the early life of Eleanor Roosevelt; and discovered exemplary leaders such as Oliver Wendell Holmes, Clara Barton, and Sojourner Truth.

Imagine my delight in learning that one of the public libraries chosen by the author of this book was my own Otis Library, founded by and still run as a non-profit organization by citizens of Norwich. It was a surprise to discover that Otis once had a branch library. Like so many branch libraries of today, this branch library, located in the village of Falls Mills, was established to serve a special population of immigrants, the young individuals who had relocated to Norwich from French Canada to work in the mills. As you read the stories of these sixteen libraries, or consider the story of your own public library, be prepared for your own discoveries.

The history of public libraries in the United States mirrors and supports the history of democracy in America. The establishment of public libraries in New England laid the foundation for the library as a place in its community where its residents would find resources for self-directed learning; for information about the community, national and world events; and current periodicals and newspapers. As communities have changed and evolved so has the public library.

Leaders of public libraries, in New England and across the nation, recognize and embrace the need to plan for the future. One established and important resource for this work has been Rising to the Challenge: Re-Envisioning Public Libraries, a project of The Aspen Institute, supported by the Gates Foundation. I had the privilege to serve as a consultant to The Aspen Institute on this project and through this work was introduced to Thomas Johnson as he began his effort on writing *Common Place.* Some libraries described in this volume are among the many who have used the tools and approaches we developed to engage their communities, boards of library trustees, and library staff in reimagining the public library for the future.

When I was elected to serve as the 2012–2013 president of the American Library Association, I chose to focus on two primary areas, the promise of libraries in transforming their communities and leadership development. The stories of the libraries featured in *Common Place* include descriptions of how and why the library was created and contributed to the development of its community. They also tell how important today the work of the library director is in providing the leadership necessary to respond to change and to move the organization forward. Library leaders and members of their boards of trustees will find information and ideas that will serve as lessons for today and planning for the future.

Library administrators and other senior leaders, along with the members of their library boards have an important responsibility to ensure effective and sustainable stewardship of these important community assets and resources. Their work includes being strong and successful advocates for funding sustainability; ensuring that the library has the resources it needs to maintain essential services, programs, and operations; and making sure the residents of the community know about and use this valuable resource.

I am today honored to serve as the Chairperson of the Connecticut State Library Board and the State Library's mission captures very well and succinctly the important work of libraries — to preserve the past and to inform the future. This applies to other libraries, large and small. *Common Place* provides an excellent history of public libraries in New England. Each profile concludes with a description of the future for that library. The individual descriptions are interesting as projections for that library. Together they make a very useful set of possibilities for any public library.

Community leaders and policy makers face a myriad of problems and challenges in developing our communities to be places that enable residents to thrive and have meaningful lives. As these leaders strive to find solutions, it is essential that the role and contribution of the public library be understood and strengthened in this work. Library leaders and library boards of trustees have important roles to play. The public library is a place that welcomes everyone and serves a variety of needs and interests. It also provides a digital platform to ensure access to the broad range of information resources and is staffed by experts who know how to distinguish fact from fiction and ensure accuracy of information.

The public library is the cornerstone of our democracy. The network of public libraries in New England and across our nation is a foundation for the strong social infrastructure that is needed and desired to ensure our future. Thomas Johnson understands this and has produced a set of profiles to educate us about the history of public libraries in New England. In doing so, he has given us a preview of the future and hope for our democracy, all from a deeper understanding of how the public library history and experience centered on New England but relevant for the rest of the United States has shaped the current situation and will influence the future.

*Maureen Sullivan*
Chair, Connecticut State Library Board and President,
American Library Association (2012–2013)

# Preface

IT MUST BE ADMITTED AT THE OUTSET, I AM A BOOK LOVER and thus fond of libraries. My first memories of going to the local public library are when I was four or five years old. It became a weekly ritual for me and my mother and sister, and there I encountered Dr. Seuss books and other children's classics like *Goodnight Moon* and *Charlotte's Web*. I remember the peculiar smell of that library. The decaying of all that paper, glue, and ink has a fragrance like no other, which I grew to love. I also remember being told that I had to keep my voice down, not easy for anyone that age, and I remember the feeling I got from the stern but understanding look the librarians gave me when I transgressed from time to time. I remember the pride of having my first library card. For many youngsters this is the first membership in any group larger than the immediate family; that is, a community. It was my first engagement with civil society, although I didn't realize it at the time, and yet, I felt the honor, the duty, it was to be part of something I sensed to be so sacred.

As I advanced through my early years, I read a lot and spent much of my time in musty school libraries with nary a computer much less the internet. In elementary school we used a card catalogue with index cards written out in the loopy script of librarians and teachers of that era. In my high school library's assortment of career reference books, I read about professions and chose my own — or at least first — career. In college I spent leisurely evenings in the campus library poring over art history books, both for class and for the visual pleasure of it. In graduate school, where I had serious research and writing to do, I spent countless hours working the microfiche card catalogues in the many libraries scattered around the large campus. I will never forget my time at the Widener, situated prominently on the main campus quad, searching among the "vast and cavernous" stacks for obscure titles amidst the dim light and silence. I realize now that it was so pleasurable in part because it seemed, unconsciously, like being back in the womb where a warm, protective covering muffled the senses and the outside world was there but at a safe distance away.

A professional career as a United States Foreign Service Officer took me away from libraries, and I missed them acutely, along with regular access to NPR, the PBS NewsHour, and decent bagels. Had to make-do with sharing dog-eared books with other expats, the BBC World Service, and local comfort foods. My wife, Michele, and I established a book club in Tegucigalpa, Honduras. We met in our living room, with French doors open to the patio and our yellow-naped amazon parrot strolling in and out. Although the bird liked being around people, it was mute, so fortunately added nothing to the often-lively discussion. In those pre-online shopping days, we ordered books to be delivered through the Embassy diplomatic pouch directly from the publishers. Zora Neale Hurston's *Their Eyes Were Watching God* was a real hit. When we transferred between posts, our book collection constituted a good portion of our household-effects weight allowance.

When I retired in 2012, after twenty-five years with the U.S. Agency for International Development, we decided it was finally time to settle down in a house somewhere outside the Washington, DC, bubble, and a town in New England was at the top of list. We were attracted to the idea of a sense of community or place, the region's local democracy, town meeting traditions, and the possibility of involvement with civil society in our community. We settled in Amherst, Massachusetts, a college town with an engaging civic spirit, purchasing an 1860 farmhouse a short walk from the South Amherst Common with its church, school, and public library branch. In the months that followed we investigated the surrounding areas, especially the Berkshires to the west. We took road trips throughout New England to visit friends or just explore. I saw a lot of small towns in western Massachusetts and northern Connecticut as I searched for streams with native trout to satisfy my newfound passion for fly-fishing. I explored places like West

Cornwall, Northampton, Litchfield, Dover, Deerfield, New Hartford, Belchertown, Lisbon, Florida, Angola, and Peru—names that traced back to England or another place of origin.

Before joining Foreign Service, I practiced landscape architecture and urban design. As a result, as I explored Amherst and other towns, I noticed the typical arrangement of many traditional New England towns. There was a town common where livestock once grazed, and around that were situated prominent public structures including the church(es), school, town hall, post office, and often the public library. I noticed that the library was often the most architecturally distinguished, if not largest of all these structures. In some very small towns, the library was the only public building of significance—and nearly all of these towns had a library. Why was this? It dawned on me that it said something about the value placed on the public library by town leaders and the community at large. I wanted to learn more and understand better how public libraries have served as the embodiment of much of what is best about America.

As my research grew, particularly involving the case studies contained in the book, I began to look beyond their physical manifestation to the role they have played in culture, society, and even politics as civic mediating institutions across America. I began to wonder: What role might libraries have, today and in the future, in addressing what some current commentators have characterized as fracturing or alienation within American society?

# Introduction — A Place of Civic and Moral Values

The title of this book, *Common Place,* is an intentional play on words. The phrase itself refers to the ubiquity of public libraries across the land, and common as a noun the town common, the location of many early New England libraries. The phrase is also synonymous with another similar term, common ground, the opinions or interests shared by each of two or more parties. Public libraries are a place in the local community where people can pursue common interests. It is a place where common folks can connect. It is not surprising to learn that the Latin root of both common and community is *communis.* Within the communities of New England, public libraries are both commonplace and a common ground, but as *Common Place* will illustrate, their historic impact and future potential are far from mundane.

Public libraries in New England have a key place in America. This too is commonplace; so much started in this region. The second group of English settlers, the Pilgrims, landed at Plymouth, Massachusetts, in 1620. They brought the first manifestation of civil society in the New World in the form of the town meeting, and they established the first institution of higher education, Harvard College, in 1636, with the first library of any type in the Americas and, two years later, the first printing press. The American Industrialization Revolution began in 1790 in the Blackstone River Valley spanning the border of Rhode Island and Massachusetts. The first public library opened nearby in Franklin, Massachusetts, that very same year. These historic events are not coincidental, as the story told in *Common Place* illustrates.

*Common Place* is not just a history of public libraries in New England, although that is certainly part of the story the book tells. Other recent works, particularly Wayne A. Wiegand's *Part of Our Lives:*

*A People's History of the American Public Library*, does this well on a national level, albeit if focused somewhat narrowly.[1] *Common Place* seeks to take a broader view in terms of covering history, current use, and the future, and in each tying the public library to the broader civic and moral culture in New England and by extension America. Wiegand writes that in the early 1800s social libraries "shaped the civic culture evolving around them." I argue this dynamic worked both ways: Civic and moral culture of the time both shaped and helped to prompt the rise of America's first public libraries. This cultural influence ranged from the Puritans in New England to the later Progressive Era, which was national in scope. Furthermore, I believe this two-way dynamic is still at work today. This is because both in the past and in current times the public library is a manifestation of civil society, whether a local government or nonprofit voluntary association runs the library. This view and emphasis set *Common Place* apart from other public library stories.

The book explores who created America's first public libraries and why they did so, and how these reasons reflected many of the civic and moral values of the time. These include the value placed on knowledge and learning as a key foundation stone of the new, growing American society, as well as the egalitarian sense that citizens were to share knowledge and learning widely. Public libraries intended to help create better, more informed citizens through supporting widespread literacy, while at the same time providing a wholesome alternative to vices of the time such as gambling and drinking. It is significant that ordinary people—teachers, the clergy, businessmen, farmers—started all the early libraries in New England through efforts of civil society and not government.

It is important to note that the public library story presented in *Common Place* is widespread in New England due to two key factors. First, the earliest public libraries reflected the civic and moral values of the time (shortly after the United States gained its independence until roughly the Civil War). This corresponds to the first five library vignettes contained in Section II. These free public libraries started during the period are common in New England. Elsewhere in America social libraries and circulating or subscription libraries prevailed, like the lyceums found in a number of major cities in the eastern United States. The second factor is related to the first because the libraries also reflected the culture and values of the people who established them. The 1771 constitution of the of social library in Salisbury, Connecticut, stated the rationale for establishing the body as the "promotion of Virtue, Education and Learning, and ... the discouragement of Vice and Immorality." These sentiments were particularly widespread in New England, home of the Puritans and their descendants, and the early public libraries established during this time reflected these values, including what became the Scoville Memorial Library in Salisbury itself (see case study in Section II).

Another common theme was youth. The founders of the two early public libraries in Salisbury and Peterborough, New Hampshire, had both already established juvenile libraries in those respective towns. The primary focus of these efforts was young men, due both to the concern with vice[2] and a desire to create more educated and effective workers. The libraries did not completely ignore young women in the early days, at least when they formed a significant portion of the workforce, as the case of the McArthur Library in Biddeford, Maine, illustrates. Scholars view Horace Mann, born in Franklin, Massachusetts, as the father of public education in America, and Mann was a strong supporter of a free public library. He said, "Had I the power, I would scatter libraries over the whole land, as the sower sows his wheat field" (Peters and Santaro, 1). Mann recognized the fact that while the number of social and circulating/subscription libraries was growing, their elitist nature and cost precluded the poor, including youth, from widely utilizing them. Andrew Carnegie, arguably the greatest supporter of public libraries in American history, was in this precise situation as a young man in Pittsburgh (see Appendix IV).

*Common Place* also examines the evolution over time of the conception of literacy and the public library's key role in promoting it, whether literacy meant only reading, as was traditionally the case, or the broader view of the term increasingly used today. When some of the early capitalists in New England supported the creation of public libraries (and several cases of this are documented in *Common Place*), it was in large part to promote functional literacy; their workforce, made up primarily of young women from rural communities and later immigrants, needed to learn to read.[3] The future of the public library, as the goal statement of the Peterborough (NH) Town Library states, is to promote literacy "in all its forms." What forms this "broad literacy"[4] includes depends to a degree on the needs of the local community, but it typically covers financial and IT knowledge, and even the ability to distinguish between fact and fiction in this age of data overload and "alternative facts." Such literacy is of course valuable both to individuals and society at large.

*Common Place* has three sections that together tell a story that began well over 200 years ago and projects into the future of what the public library can and should be. The sections cover the history of the public library, vignettes of the past and present of sixteen libraries across New England, and the future of the institution as part of America's "social infrastructure."[5] Each section is likely to be of particular interest to different readers. A people who love libraries, or more broadly books, will find pleasure in the broader history offered in Section I, while those who enjoy learning about local history, particularly in New England, will especially appreciate Section II. Section III is likely to appeal to forward-thinking advocates who want to consider America's past, the challenges and opportunities of the present, and leverage that knowledge for America's future.

Whether it involves this broad literacy or acquisition of special knowledge, *Common Place* argues that public libraries also have a greater role to play in supporting lifelong-learning efforts by community members, whether linked to mid-life workforce skills improvement or a member of America's growing elderly population tied to nothing more than learning for the sake of learning. What public libraries have going for them in this regard is their "commonplaceness" across America, thus providing easy access to resources, and ability to serve as a local platform for obtaining written materials from elsewhere in statewide library systems, and the internet with the provision of curation services from a Reference Librarian, if requested by a patron.

Thus, argues the book, the future public library should be a civil society grounded social institution dedicated to promotion of literacy in all its forms and a local platform for lifelong living efforts. Both should be offered in ways that promote engagement of users with the community, and among each other regardless of age, gender, ethnicity or political views. This would help stem the sense of alienation found in too many communities and further contribute to wellbeing and opportunities for all Americans, and especially those living in the towns and rural areas featured in *Common Place.*

The first section of the book briefly covers the history of the library from antiquity, and then moves to the evolution of the public library in America, the first anywhere in the world. The section notes the first public libraries in America, not all of which are in New England, as well as the establishment of the largest library in the world: The Library of Congress. It is notable if not surprising that the father of the public library was none other than Benjamin Franklin. While he is not widely known for this feat, it is yet another "invention" that Franklin gave to the world.

The section then turns to a discussion of the relationship, from a historic perspective, of public libraries, American values, and civil culture reflected in New England communities. Next, the section explores the role of civil society and civic philanthropy, highlighted by Andrew Carnegie's support of creating public libraries across America around 1900, which was late by New England standards. As the case studies in Section II document, Carnegie mimicked, on a large scale, what businessmen in New England had been doing for years on a local scale. The first section concludes with a brief discussion of public library architecture and site selection within the townscape of communities in New England, and how this choice reflected the value of the institution—both to the community and in some cases individual interest.

The final part of Section I explores the contemporary nexus between civil society and public libraries. What most readers of this book, or the general public for that matter, do not realize is that aside from their historic association today, many public libraries in New England are operated not by local governments but rather civil society organizations. Of the sixteen case studies contained in Section II of the book, half of the public libraries are run by nongovernmental organizations. Even the town- or city-run libraries operate on civil society principles with autonomous boards of trustees.

The discussion begins with a definition and overview of civil society history, which in many ways is yet another American creation. This assertion was documented in what came to be an influential book, *Democracy in America*, authored by a Frenchman, Alexis de Tocqueville, who visited America in the 1830s. While Tocqueville did not use the term "civil society" or mention public libraries, his profound appreciation of Americans' associational efforts and accomplishments is clear. By the time he wrote his words, four of the public libraries highlighted in the case studies had already been established, and they serve as a prime example of both efforts and accomplishments. The discussion then turns to the contemporary debate between the political left and right concerning the importance and role of civil society and its institutions today, and particularly the widely accepted linkage between a strong civil society and both individual and community well-being. This issue is explored at length in the final section of the book.

In Section II, sixteen public libraries throughout New England are featured and for each its past and present stories are told (see Appendix II for the listing along with information on the communities in which they are located). Each case study illustrates major themes of the book. These libraries were not selected randomly, but rather purposively based on several criteria. Four of the libraries were selected on the basis of their historic nature, reflecting firsts in New England or America as a whole. The remainder were selected more randomly, albeit with diversity in mind. Some were selected because they are located in small cities that once had thrived due to their early manufacturing industries. Others are located in rural areas or villages. Some are located in what are today well-endowed communities, while others are in locations that face challenges in terms of livelihoods, well-being, and social capital. One community in the latter group was selected because it was found in research covered in the final section of *Common Place* to have very low levels of community well-being. The case study question explores the connection, if any, between the mitigation of community distress and the public library.

Each case study begins with scene-setting through a historic and contemporary look at the village, town, or small city in which the public library is located. Historical facts and figures are presented along with current demographic figures. The historical story of the library's creation is then presented, based on archival research and interviews with librarians and local historians. Next is a description of the current use and services offered by the institution. This information came from a standard questionnaire used in the interviews with the library director, a member of the library board, and in some cases a representative of the local "friends of the library" group. Questionnaire answers were also used for completing the final part of the case study on the future of the library, along with information from any available strategic plans and community surveys.

The book concludes in Section III with consideration of the future of the public library, not just in New England but across America. The section draws on discussions with several library directors that happened while conducting the case studies. These library scientists in Montpelier, Vermont; Lexington, Massachusetts; Biddeford, Maine; and Peterborough, New Hampshire are working closely with their boards and community stakeholders to set an exemplary vision for the future for their libraries. Discussions with the State Librarians of Vermont and Connecticut and a past president of the American Library Association, who is now respected consultant in the field, were also very useful in informing the contents of the section.

Discussion of the future starts by looking back to the golden age of public library creation, which coincided with what is known as the Progressive Era in American history. What prompted the era and how the values reflected at the time by the Progressives is evidenced in their support for community, civil society, and public libraries, and whether similar factors present today, including the crises in many communities and well-documented decay in civil society, could lead to an analogous era in the near future.

The section turns to a review of survey results from Americans concerning their library use and support—which is widespread. The section presents survey data by the four major age groups or generations designated by social scientists: silent, baby boomer, Generation X, and millennials. The section highlights the pioneering work on civil society and social capital by Robert D. Putnam in his book *Bowling Alone: The Collapse and Revival of American Community* and others. It is not surprising that Putnam is a great supporter of the public library, and indeed he recently appeared at a community fundraising event for the Peterborough Town Library, near his home in Jaffrey, New Hampshire. His research, which found that twenty years ago social capital levels in New England were the highest in America, is compared and contrasted with more recent books, including *The Fractured Republic* and *Alienated America*, by conservative commentators Yuval Levin and Timothy P. Carney, respectively, on the same general topic.

Following that, there are related recent research findings from Gallup-Sharecare and the nongovernmental organizations Opportunity Nation and Child Trends that measure community well-being and opportunity generated by nationwide, multi-year surveys. These results also show that the region with the highest state-level well-being scores is New England, with Vermont placing first in the nation both in the well-being and opportunity indices scores. This data is then, for the first time, compared with public library statistics from the annual nationwide survey conducted by the United States Institute for Museum and Library Services (IMLS). The correlation between state-level well-being and opportunity and public library support and use is astonishing, both at the high-end in New England and the low-end among states in the South. Causation is not established, but the evidence documented in *Common Place* points to a very strong connection between public libraries, social capital, and well-being.

The section then discusses broad socioeconomic trends in America, including the aging population and what had been, until recently, longer average life spans, as well as changes in the labor market and workforce brought about by increasing automation and artificial intelligence. All these trends have a bearing on the future of the public library as an increasingly important resource for individual lifelong learning efforts, either for pleasure or necessity. The section highlights the provocative idea of displacement in the labor force leading to widespread worker redundancy and the alternative of a new class of lifelong learners, and it also explores the meaning of "literacy for all" in terms of possible future nontraditional literacy needs.

Section III concludes with a final future scenario: for public libraries to serve in this age of internet overload and "alternative facts" as they have in the past, as a repository of curated information and facts. Anyone who has dealt with a helpful and knowledgeable reference librarian can appreciate this value. Surveys indicate a current and future demand for this type of service, to include internet curation assistance, including from millennials and particularly members of minority groups.

In summary, the three main sections of *Common Place* cover the past, present and future of public libraries. While the book is intended to be read in that chronological sequence, some readers may wish to begin in the middle with the case studies and then explore how the broader past history and prospects for the future reflect on the public library cases presented. In whatever way the book is approached, what it convincingly illustrates is that public libraries have and continue to exemplify core American civic values and culture. Indeed, the Library Company, America's first subscription library established by Benjamin Franklin in 1731, is considered America's oldest cultural institution.[6] Perhaps most importantly for the future, data indicates support for and use of public libraries appears correlated with individual well-being and enhanced social capital. These foundational institutions may continue to provide an opportunity to remedy important challenges today facing American society — just as they have done in the past.

# SECTION I:

# The Library in History and New England

LIBRARIES IN ONE FORM OR ANOTHER DATE TO ANTIQUITY as repositories of knowledge. The most famous ancient library was the Great Library of Alexandria, established in 300 BC by the Greeks. Although open to the members of the public with proper qualifications, it served more as an archive for the royalty and the scholars that served them. The books of that era were scrolls. The Romans continued to establish libraries, but not in great numbers, and all the libraries were actually private collections. The spread of Christianity and the desire for increased literacy (to read the Bible) led monasteries to create and maintain libraries of handwritten religious manuscripts during the Dark Ages. During the Renaissance private collections again grew, in large part among classics scholars, and early universities, such as Oxford, began to develop libraries after 1400. Gutenberg invented moveable type in the mid-1400s, and by the time America, particularly New England, was being settled in the 1600s, the popularity of private libraries surged, commensurate with the literacy of the educated, who were usually upper-class males.

## Evolution of the Public Library in America

The first library in North America began in New England with a donation of 400 books, many written in Latin or Greek, by clergyman John Harvard to America's first university, established in 1636. (See Appendix I for a timeline of public library history discussed here and in the Section II case studies.) The founders expressed their gratitude by naming the institution after him. During the 1600s and early 1700s libraries in America, like Europe, were essentially private book collections in the hands of individuals, typically scholars or intellectuals, or located at a college or university like Harvard.

An exhaustive study of all types of libraries found that the number in America prior to 1786 had been at one point or another just over 300 with the largest number, 120, in the New England region. Of those 58 were in Connecticut and 43 in Massachusetts. In terms of the former, according to library historian Jesse Shera a library was established in 1737 to serve the adjoining towns of Guilford, Saybrook, Killingworth and Lyme. In terms of the latter, by the 1670s, libraries, although not public, had been established in Boston and Concord. New England also had the majority (estimated at over 60 percent) of booksellers and publishers during the Colonial period (Shera, 49).[7] There were 83 libraries in the mid-Atlantic region with 41 in Pennsylvania. The south-Atlantic region had 99 libraries, including 41 in Maryland (McMullen, 17).[8]

Although John Harvard may have established the first library in America, there is no dispute that the father of the public library in America, and indeed the world, was Benjamin Franklin. In 1731, at age twenty-five, he led the establishment of America's first lending or circulating library in Philadelphia. The Library Company of Philadelphia was founded as a subscription service by Franklin and other members of a gentlemen's club he had formed in 1727 of "like minded aspiring artisans and tradesmen who hoped to improve themselves while they improved their community." Previously they had traded volumes from their personal collections, but henceforth the library imported books from England for subscribers, but not the general public. Starting with around fifty members investing forty shillings, with another ten for a new book purchase, the library was open one day a week on the club premises and later in the state house.

The Library Company served as the de facto Library of Congress from the Revolutionary War until 1800 when the nation's capital moved to Washington, DC (more on the Library of Congress to follow). The Library Company eventually grew into the American Philosophical Society, and the success of the lending library caused other groups, such as in the nearby town of Darby, to replicate the subscription-lending system.

Following the Revolutionary War interest in libraries increased. Historians believe one reason for this was that in a republic books and learning should be widely available (McMullen, 19). In the period 1781–85, 29 libraries were in existence in New England and the mid- and south-Atlantic regions. In the next five-year period, the number jumped to 67; between 1791–95 the number rose significantly again to 157, virtually all of which were located in the northeast.

Public libraries can be broadly defined as local institutions offering access to books without charge to a large proportion of the population in a small geographic area. In the book, *Foundation of the Public Library: The Origins of the Public Library Movement in New England, 1629–1855*, Jessie G. Shera analyzed conditions and social values which existed during the period. Among those identified: local interest in educational materials beyond those available in elementary schools; a degree of local pride in the community; and available resources and a willingness to tax residents to support a library. Of the just over 400 public libraries Shera identified during this period, roughly 250 were in New England. Massachusetts had 172, about six times as many as in any other state.[9] While Shera associated public libraries established during this period with town governments, many were in fact established and run by non-governmental associations (as were social libraries), albeit often with some degree of local government support (Shera, 200–44).

Determining what was the first public library established in America is more difficult than one would think. What makes a library *public*? Is it a collection of books, a library building, or both that constitute a library's establishment? Does a private book collection or subscription service become a public library if members or patrons can join from the general public? Does being open to the general public at little or nominal cost suffice, or must the institution be tax-supported to qualify?

There are five main contenders for this honor, three of them in New England and two connected directly to Benjamin Franklin. The Darby Free Library outside of Philadelphia bills itself as the "oldest library in the United States in *continuous* service" (italics added). Note that it does not claim to be the oldest public library. It started, following Franklin's Library Company of Philadelphia, as the Darby Library Company in 1743 as a subscription society that lasted until 1898 when it opened to the public. The company constructed its own library building in 1872. The four earliest public libraries in New England are featured in Section II, located in Franklin, Massachusetts; Salisbury, Connecticut; Lexington, Massachusetts; and Peterborough, New Hampshire.

The Franklin Public Library is widely considered by historians as America's first public library. In 1778 the Commonwealth of Massachusetts incorporated the town and changed the old name of Exeter to Franklin. In return, town residents requested Dr. Franklin donate a bell for the town's church steeple. He responded that "sense was preferable to sound" and instead offered books from his private library. In 1790 the town meeting voted to lend the books to all Franklin residents free of charge. Thus, the term free library came into usage, predating the term *public library*. A local family, the Rays, gave the town a building for the library in 1904. Today the Franklin book collection is still in the library's reading room.

The Peterborough Town Library in New Hampshire was established in 1833 and is considered by town residents and others the oldest tax-supported public library in *continuous operation*. The founders purchased the original book collection with funds from the state literary fund — the first such body in the nation. In fact, in 1849 the state established the first law in the nation authorizing towns to raise money to establish and maintain their public libraries, prompted by the establishment of the Peterborough Town Library.

Lexington, Massachusetts, is renowned for being the site of the beginning of the Revolutionary War, where the minutemen first confronted British troops on the town common. It's public library, the

Cary Memorial, traces its roots back to 1827 when the town meeting voted to establish a juvenile library and to raise sixty dollars to purchase books by a tax on residents. This appears to make Lexington the oldest tax-supported, contentiously open public library in Massachusetts if not the United States, preceding Peterborough by a few years.

Based on historical documentation there is no dispute that the first tax-supported public library in America began in 1810 in Salisbury, Connecticut. However, that town's library, founded in 1803 as the Bigham Library for Youth, did not remain in continuous operation like the public libraries in Lexington and Peterborough.

While not the focus of this book, two other public libraries in America bear mention. The first, cited earlier, is the Library of Congress established by Congress in 1800. The oldest federal cultural institution in the United States, the library housed its initial collection in the United States Capitol, but when the British burned the building in the War of 1812, the books were lost. In 1815 Congress purchased the private library of Thomas Jefferson for $24,000 and relocated the nearly 6,500-volume collection from Monticello to serve as the new foundation of what has become a national treasure. The library's collection was in the rebuilt Capitol until the library's current building was constructed in 1893.

The Library of Congress is the largest library in the world today, and from the beginning, parts of its collection have been available to members of the public. In this sense, it can actually be considered the oldest tax-supported public library in America.[10] The second public library worth mentioning is the first tax-supported public library in a large municipality, Boston, which was established in 1848—roughly twenty years after the citizens of Lexington, Massachusetts, located only fifteen miles away, voted to tax themselves to create their public library.

## Public Libraries, American Values, and Civil Culture

From the beginning books and libraries reflected the value Americans placed on knowledge and education, which was strongly held by various denominational groups such as the Puritans, Quakers, and First Baptists led by Roger Williams in Rhode Island. However, this value was secular, transcended religion (see, for example, the case of the first public library in Franklin, Massachusetts), and continued to animate the establishment of public libraries during their golden age and particularly the Progressive Era of American history.

Aside from the value of knowledge alone, libraries also become associated with classical culture in the 1700s. Building on this connotation, a number of early learned societies in New England named their subscription libraries *Athenaeum,* after the famous school in ancient Rome established by Emperor Hadrian. Most remain membership based, such as the Redwood Library and Athenæum in Newport, Rhode Island, while some have become public libraries such as the Berkshire Athenaeum in Pittsfield, Massachusetts.

In 1826 a new type of civil society association formed, called the *lyceum*. Begun in Massachusetts, the lyceum had three purposes: the provision of adult education through discussion and lectures; improvement of instruction in public school; and the establishment of libraries and museums. Within a decade there were said to be nearly 3,000 of them and many in the period 1830–50 created what amounted to social libraries, albeit with an objective of self-education (Shera, 226). Charging audiences for lectures was the primary means to generate the resources to purchase books. As the movement petered out during the latter half of the 19th century book collections were usually donated to the growing number of public libraries (McMullen, 94–95).

Up until about 1820, libraries were, with a few exceptions, created by groups for reasons largely involving self-interest. These constituted the private social libraries, church libraries and specialized libraries held by professional associations.[11] During this decade, however, voluntary associations began to establish libraries for the benefit of disadvantaged groups including hospital and asylum patients, low-skill workers and youth. This took place primarily in northeastern states and cities (McMullen, 62). The altruistic concern for welfare remained a motivating force during the remainder of the 19th century, reaching a climax during the Progressive Era.

During the latter half of the 1800s many reform-minded Americans thought literacy, books, and reading were a mark of good character, morals, and self-improvement, and that they were an antidote for vices such as alcohol, gambling, and womanizing. This is a reason why during this period public library supporters were often associated with the church or women interested in improving the behavior of their husbands or sons.[12] It is one reason that by the late-1800s public tax dollars established and maintained many public libraries, and today libraries are not just the preserve of the wealthy or scholarly book collector. This belief is also the basis for Andrew Carnegie's largess in establishing a public library system across America, particularly in underserved geographic areas and small towns—both with fewer public services and cultural amenities. Carnegie Public Library (Turners Falls, Massachusetts) and Athol Public Library (Athol, Massachusetts) are two of the three such Carnegie libraries featured in this book, and the appendix has more information about the significance of Carnegie's philanthropy more than a century ago.

The term *civil society* refers to a group or community of citizens linked by common interests and collective activity or action, distinct from the state or government and for-profit business. Although the term is widely used today, the concept dates back to ancient Greece. Alex de Tocqueville, a French aristocrat and an astute early observer of civil society in America, described and admired the widespread presence of civil society when he visited, and subsequently described it in his 1835 book, *Democracy in America*. This is the citizen associative life, which includes the bowling leagues once found across America that Harvard Professor Robert D. Putnam described in his noted 1995 article in the *Journal of Democracy* and his book *Bowling Alone: America's Declining Social Capital*.

Subscription libraries, sometimes referred to as lending societies or social libraries, were like the town of Franklin's, the type of civil society organization that caught the eye of Tocqueville, although they were not unknown in England and other parts of Europe. Unlike elsewhere, American civil society led the establishment of public libraries as is illustrated by the case studies in this book. That this largely happened in New England is no coincidence. Not only one of the earliest settled regions of America, but the home of the common (a town layout brought from England), and the town meeting, particularly unique to America. Today the town meeting is a formal part of government in many New England local jurisdictions, but in the early days it had more of a civil society cast. Town residents came together on a regular basis to consider matters of common interest and decide courses of action. Tocqueville wrote extensively about what he termed the "township," noting that they were, "... the only association so well rooted in nature that wherever men assemble it forms itself" (Tocqueville, 62).

Establishing a public library was a prime example of common interest, as happened regularly throughout New England. (See, for example, the early cases of Salisbury, Lexington, and Peterborough where town meeting members voted to establish libraries *and* tax themselves for book purchase in the process.) In many other cases, public libraries were established by library associations, early civil society organizations that flourished in many New England towns. These types of civil society organizations still exist and flourish throughout much of New England, perhaps surprisingly given Putnam's thesis that civil society and social capital are on the decline across America.

Today's public libraries, which are usually a valued service of the local government, were thus typically civil society creations. Moreover, public libraries continue to be operated in many cases by civil society organizations, generally a library association, without any public support other than some funding. In other words, while many Americans assume public libraries are a local government service, many are in fact nongovernmental organizations. Examples include several cases featured in the book, and other institutions such as the Athenaeum established on Nantucket Island as a subscription library in 1834 and made a public library in 1900. All such libraries are overseen by a local board of trustees and not the local town or city. This is common among libraries in New England, where they provide an early and contemporary example of a public-private (nonprofit) partnership. In 2017 of all public libraries in Maine, 57 percent were civil society organizations, including those in the largest towns and cities. Section II features two of them. It is not surprising that libraries have, to this day, relied on community volunteers to support professional staff. As Putnam and others have widely noted, such volunteerism helps builds social capital within communities.

Public libraries also reflected the American trait of civic philanthropy, as the early collections consisted almost exclusively of donated private book collections. These libraries used grants to purchase new books (initially from England) and construct purpose-built structures as the nascent libraries outgrew their first homes in churches, private houses (often occupied by clergymen), shops, or a room in town hall. It was unusual for the costs for establishing a public library not to be a combination of public funds and private contributions, even in the case of the later Carnegie libraries, which as a condition of the grant required public support.

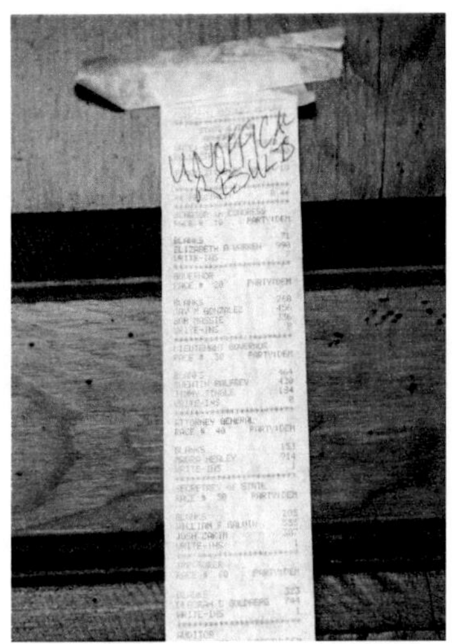

Unofficial voting results taped to the wall outside the community hall of the Munson Memorial Library in South Amherst, MA.

Reflecting civic values, many communities used, and continue to use, public libraries for community meetings and places to vote—perhaps the most important of all civic duties. The idea of a *lending library*, first established in America, as opposed to reading books *in situ* within the library building, reflected intercommunity trust and social capital—foundations of the civil society and values noted by Tocqueville and later highlighted by Putnam and others.

## Public Library Site Selection Within the Townscape

The physical location of the public library, particularly in small towns throughout New England, illustrates its importance as a symbol of civic values and pride. Libraries were often sited literally at the center of community life around the town common or on Main Street near the town hall or community meeting house. The library, more than any other public building, reflects the value placed by the community on knowledge and a civil society in the classic sense of the term. This siting had both symbolic and practical value, as it permitted convenient access to books and therefore, literacy and learning. Before stand-alone library buildings became common in the late 1800s, residents of a town could at times shop at the general store, pick up their mail at the post office, and check out a book from the public library—all in the same location.

The Munson Memorial Library in South Amherst, Massachusetts, is such an example, sited on the town common next to the church on land donated for the purpose by a civil leader. The Cary Memorial Library in Lexington, Massachusetts, is at the tip of the town common—among the most well-known in New England—just opposite the iconic minuteman statue commemorating the beginning of the Revolutionary War. The small library in Guilford, Vermont, is adjacent to the meeting house in the center of the rural community. In

The Munson Memorial Library adjacent to the Congregational Church with Fiddler's Green to the left foreground.

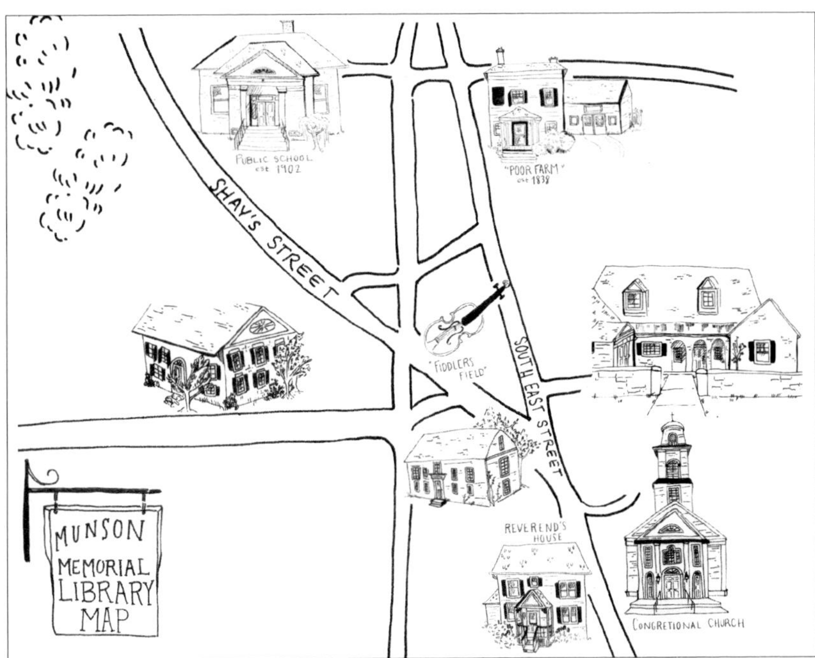


Sketch plan drawn by Grace Desmarais illustrating how the Munson Memorial Library in Amherst, MA (right center) is situated within the local townscape. Before the current structure was built in the 1930s the South Amherst Library Association book collection was housed in the general store/post office (left center).

such locations the new libraries joined earlier structures of civic significance—the church, school, and the hall used for the region's renowned town meetings. In fact, some define the New England town common as an open space surrounded by such social institutions.[13]

In New England towns without a proper common, the library building was invariably placed in a site of honor along Main Street. Given its hilly topography, the town of Conway, Massachusetts, has no commons. Architects instead sited the public library at the end of a stunning view corridor seen from Route 116, the de facto town main street, as it approaches from the Berkshires to the west. The architects also ensured through careful siting that the library entrance, flanked by a stunning façade of locally quarried stone, basks in light at sundown, providing a rich, warm glow in the otherwise often gloomy New England winter. In cases such as Conway, the public library was often

The building exterior viewed from Conway's main street, Route 116.

the largest, most architecturally distinguished and significant public structure in a New England town.

Classical architectural styles used for the early libraries reflect back to the Roman athenaeum, as well as the idea of refinement and culture. Whereas most buildings in a New England town were wooden structures, most libraries were built of stone or brick for a sense of value and permanence. This material also helps protect irreplaceable library collections against the threat of town-wide fires, which were not uncommon in the past. While more costly, stone or brick served as insurance to better safeguard an important public asset.

The architectural and site designs commonly included spaces for not only books and reading, but community meetings and other public functions including dances, theater, and even kindergarten classes and small outside playgrounds. Not surprisingly, libraries provide a home for many community book clubs—the successors to literary societies of past eras, such as Benjamin Franklin's. Libraries today also connect local patrons with the broader world of books, knowledge and people through personal computers, internet access, and wide library networks, not an insignificant public service in isolated and/or disadvantaged communities, of which New England, like the rest of America, has its share.

## Civil Society and Public Libraries

Public libraries in New England, and thus America, began within what is now known as *civil society*. It is important to explore these roots not only to understand the genesis of the public library but because today many public libraries in America are civil society institutions.

We start the exploration with a discussion of the meaning of civil society through history and in America today where the concept is receiving renewed attention. Definitions have evolved over time. Civil society's roots, like so many other modern phenomena, go back to ancient Greece, but it is part of the human experience that predates that era and extends beyond the West to wherever humans formed societies. It connects to how individuals, families, and communities *associate* for a common interest or good among each other, outside state or governmental coercion structures that exist or monetary reward, which is the hallmark of the private sector. Individual engagement in civil society is by definition voluntary. Today it is the "third sector," beside but distinct from the state or government (i.e., the public sector) and (for-profit) business or commerce (i.e., the private sector). Today's political scientists see a healthy civil society as a key part of good governance, and most social scientists and even many political pundits view it as fundamentally important to formation of social capital, individual, and community well-being, and even economic opportunity.

Many scholars link the term *civil society* back to the thinking and writings of Aristotle, Socrates, Plato, and, in Rome, Cicero. The concept revolved around the ideas of community, the common cause and good, well-being, voluntary association, and a just and virtuous society marked by civility. For example, Plato believed that the ideal state was a just society in which people dedicate themselves to the common good and practice civic virtues of wisdom, courage, moderation, and justice. Aristotle conceived the *polis* as an "association of associations." Cicero used the Roman term, *societas civilis,* tied to the idea of a "good society" in which citizenship linked to civility, or in today's thinking, civic values. However, the distinction during this era between the state, politics, and civil society was murky as the concept of *polis* reflects. Aristotle would likely have said that the associations he referred to were political in nature. This illustrates the blurry line throughout human history between politics and nonpartisan civic associations for collective activity or action.

Not surprisingly, civil society has long been associated with classic liberal democracy; its underlying values, if not the term itself, can be found in the writings of Georg Wilhelm Friedrich Hegel, Alexis de Tocqueville, and, more recently, political scientists such as Robert A. Dahl. Hegel made the distinction between the state (macro), the family (micro), and civil society (the middle), which most observers today still view as a sound distinction. Civil society comprises the nonstate aspects of a society covering culture, rules and norms, types and character of member association, and, to an often-debated degree, its politics.

Robert A. Dahl was a political theorist and professor at Yale University who was an influential thinker on democracy, beginning in the 1960s, known in particular for his work involving pluralism. In his 1998 book, *On Democracy*, Dahl discussed the five "political institutions of a modern representative democracy." Aside from things like elections and freedom of expression, he included "associational autonomy," which gave citizens the "right" to form "relatively independent" associations or organizations, including political parties and interest groups. Dahl's focus, however, was on political associations—interest groups and political parties—which are one part, but certainly do not constitute all of civil society. He noted their importance in terms of civic education and "enlightenment," to which could be added engagement.

Dahl went on to note in his book that by the time Alexis de Tocqueville visited the United States in the 1830s, all but one of his necessary political institutions could be found—what was missing, and even today is debated, was "inclusive citizenship." Dahl highlighted the fact that Tocqueville was astounded by the multiplicity of associations he found by which Americans organized themselves for a multitude of purposes.

Other political scientists have noted Tocqueville's interest in civil society and his tying it to New England and its Puritan roots. In *Why Liberalism Failed*, Patrick J. Deneen repeats that Tocqueville found a "beautiful definition of liberty" that he drew from Cotton Mather's *The Ecclesiastical History of New England* that distinguished between liberty seen as license (individualistic being what one pleases) and free choice made on behalf of the common good. Following Tocqueville, Deneen wrote, "Democracy required the abridgement of the desires and preferences of the individual, particularly in light of an awareness of the common good that could become discernable only through ongoing interactions with fellow citizens" (Deneen, 175). If civil society ever had a creed, this could be part of it.

Decades earlier Benjamin Franklin had also been influenced by Mather's thinking and writings (in particular, *Bonifacius: Essays to Do Good*), which appears to have helped prompt Franklin's civic mindedness that resulted in the Library Company among many other, what we can term now, civil society initiatives (Shera, 31). Mather's tract called on citizens to form voluntary associations to benefit the community, and Franklin's father joined such a civil society group formed in Boston by Mather (Issacson, 26). In fact, Cotton Mather and later Benjamin Franklin more than any other single individuals helped engender and embed civil society principles in America.

Tocqueville discerned a thread between this Puritanical view of liberty and a high degree of self-governance directed at the common good in the early towns of New England. Tocqueville surmised that "the strength of free peoples resides in the local community. Local institutions are to liberty what primary school are to science: they put it within the people's reach; they teach people to appreciate its peaceful enjoyment and accustom them take use of it."

*Democracy in America* does not mention public libraries by name, but these were just the type of "associations in civil life" he was referring to.[14] At the time of his visit to America, the first civil society library association founded by Benjamin Franklin had been in existence for a century, the first public library had been established for forty years (also with Franklin's support), and town meetings in Salisbury, Lexington, and Peterborough had recently voted to support their towns' public libraries with local tax dollars. Tocqueville does devote sections of his book to the "spirit of the Township in New England" and the "use the Americans make of associations in civil life." His perceptions relate both to formation of early public libraries and their support, operation, and use today.

Tocqueville quaintly subtitles the pertinent section of *Democracy in America* in old time fashion as: "why the New England township wins the affection of the inhabitants; how municipal spirit manifests itself in New England; and what happy results it produces there." He does not distinguish in denoting "municipal institutions" between what citizens today would consider governmental or civil society. In his eyes they are all part of the township and linked to the municipal spirit, which he argues is built on independence and power. These refer to a high degree of self-governance, which gives citizens a sense of power to affect things for the common good through individual and collective action. If citizens want to support their town library, for example, check to see if there's state legislation that either supports or prohibits such an action. In the case of neither, do it anyway as the Peterborough town meeting members did in 1833.

Because the town meeting was the basis of local governance in New England and is a quintessential civil society institution that was instrumental in the formation of public libraries in the region, it is useful to learn more about them. They grew out of the most important civil society institution in early America—the church, specifically, the Congregational church established by the Puritans, who then created the town meeting to mimic the church governance system. The congregational system was based upon independence, self-support, and governance, unlike the hierarchical systems used by the Presbyterian or Episcopal polities, much less the Catholic Church in Europe. In the original open town meeting system, adult male residents played the part of members of the congregation to elect town officers and representatives, deliberate, and decide. Indeed, through these related systems, most adult males participated in both the governance of their town and church. It is important to note that while many local leaders often were involved in the governance of both, from the very start they governed independently as the case study of the Franklin Public Library involving a dispute between the congregational church and town meeting illustrates.

In writing about the use Americans make of association in civil life (i.e., civil society), Tocqueville begins by noting he is not talking about political associations (covered elsewhere in *Democracy in America*) but rather "those associations in civil life which have no political object." He notes that in America, unlike in France or England, "at the head of any new undertaking... you are sure to find an association." He lists many examples ranging from civil society organizations dedicated to commerce and industry, hospitals, "sending missionaries to the antipodes," and distributing books. Of all the evidence of democracy Tocqueville encountered during his travels in America, this civil society activity seems to have made the greatest impression on him. He concludes, "Thus the most democratic country in the world now is that in which men have in our time carried to the highest perfection the art of pursuing the common the objects of common desires and have applied this new technique to the greatest number of purposes. Is that just an accident or is there really some necessary connection between associations and equality?"

Collective action cannot be forced on individuals even for the common good, but rather citizens must learn to help each other voluntarily. Today, people undertake many such efforts through a *private voluntary organization (PVO)*, which is generally synonymous with the term *nongovernmental organization (NGO)*. Some contemporary scholars use the term mediating institutions to describe organizations of civil society to reflect their middle position in society between families or households and the state. These include such well-known local institutions as Boys & Girls Clubs of America, the YMCA or YWCA, Little League and other sporting leagues, local churches, and the public library.

Tocqueville was perceptive and also recognized an issue that still debated in America nearly 200 years later. That is the question of the role of government, vis-à-vis civil society NGOs, in the provision of common-good services. At that time, some of Tocqueville's contemporaries believed that as society advanced and became more complex, the role of governments in such service provision should increase. He disagreed, pointing out that "the more government takes the place of associations, the more will individuals lose the idea of forming associations and need the government to come to their help. That is a vicious circle of cause and effect." Tocqueville concluded, "The morals and intelligence of a democratic people would be in as much danger as its commerce and industry if ever a government wholly usurped the place of private associations." This is a view shared by many commentators, generally considered politically conservative, today.

Why is this relevant to the history of the public library in New England? Virtually all early public libraries in America were created through civil society efforts, as the case studies in this book illustrate. *In Arsenals of a Democratic Culture,* author Ditzion noted the Peterborough Town Library "is unique in that here we have an instance of what appears to be the spontaneous generation of an entirely new form. Here, without the stimulus of private donation, without permission of state legislation, without the semblance of a model in the mother country (England), a tax-supported town library was born" (Ditzion, pg. 4). What he refers to as an "entirely new form" is civil society in action. What is notable is that many public libraries, at least in New England, are still operated by civil society organizations. Even those run by the local government, be it a town or city, are required by law to have civil society features, most significantly a board of trustees whose apolitical community members are either elected or appointed voluntarily.

The Maine Library Commission defines a public library as a town department or an organization with a governing board that has adopted written bylaws, hires/appoints the library director, and prepares an annual report for publication. A public library must also have a mission statement defining the services available to the community and be supported in whole or part with public funds. According to the Maine State Library 2017 annual report, 57 percent of all public libraries in the state were legally NGOs.[15] While the proportion of NGO libraries is higher in Maine than other states in New England, the definition and requirements for a public library are virtually the same across the region and indeed America as a whole.

Public libraries are unique in that they include non-profit, NGO-run institutions which governments at all levels and citizens alike consider *public*. Indeed, not many Americans or residents of a town itself realize NGOs run many public libraries. The United States Institute for Museum and Library Services (IMLS) 2016 Annual Report contains a huge database of information on all public libraries in America. The total universe was 9,234 public library systems, of which 1,341 were operated by an "non-profit association or agency," representing nearly 15 percent of the total number. The corresponding figures for New England are higher. The fear of Tocqueville and some conservative commentators today that the state will, if allowed, usurp civil society provision of services to the public is demonstrably not true when it comes to public libraries in New England.

This is important because, as previously noted on page 17, while public libraries in New England were ahead of the curve, the main expansion of the public library system in America coincided with the Progressive Era, during which Andrew Carnegie's support of the institutions was just one important aspect. Indeed, many consider public libraries as one of the more important institutional legacies of the period. In an interesting analysis of public library development in the decades after 1890 investigators found a few key factors associated with growth of these social institutions (Kevane). The study found that a higher number of library volumes per capita (i.e., more public libraries) was associated with (more) local tax revenue per capita, (larger) proportion of the population under 18, (larger) proportion of the population that was foreign-born and the presence of a state library commission. The most salient Progressive Era reform emphases are on youth and immigrants, with both groups particularly benefitting from access to public libraries.

Political conservatives frequently point to the Progressive Era as the beginning of "big government" in America and also assert this diminished the role and number of the civil society associations Tocqueville had hailed a half-century earlier. Based on the historic records available, this is an untrue assertion. In fact, quite the opposite. The Progressive Era was the golden age of civil society association formation, including public libraries. One only need refer to Appendix III, "The Rise and Fall of Civic and Professional Associations," in Putnam's *Bowling Alone*. The founding of the majority of the "middle institutions," national in scope but all with local chapters, listed was during the Progressive Era, or between roughly 1895 and 1915. Examples include the PTA (1897), the Girl and Boy Scouts of America (1910 and 1912) and, germane to Putnam's story, the American Bowling Congress (1895). The founding of the American Library Association itself was in 1876.[16]

Contrast this odd public nature of the library with another ubiquitous community institution, the elementary or secondary school. In these cases, schools operated by either NGOs or for-profit firms are considered private, while only schools operated by the local government/ school district are considered public. Not so for libraries and in this sense, they are interesting public-private hybrid institutions.[17] This raises a number of interesting questions, with answers bearing on the vitality of local civil society, levels of social capital, and community well-being. Why have residents of some towns opted for an NGO-run public library as opposed to one operated by the town? Are there any discernable differences between the two measured by services or use? Why have public libraries operated by NGOs not been "crowded out" by the government as Tocqueville and some of today's conservative commentators feared would happen?[18]

The case studies help provide us with some of the answers. Of the sixteen public libraries included, half are NGO-operated. The size of the community does not seem to be a factor, nor does the community's socioeconomic profile. In only one instance, the Field Memorial Library in Conway, Massachusetts, did the nature of a benefactor preference have direct influence on the form of library administration. Both public libraries in New Hampshire towns are town operated, while NGOs run the two each in Connecticut, Vermont, and Maine. In Massachusetts there is an interesting mix. The reasons behind this are not clear. In questioning of past presidents of the New England Library Association and the American Library Association[19], as well as the State Librarians of Connecticut and Vermont, none could provide a definitive answer. Most surmised the differences were a result of local conditions and history, or perhaps state-level legislation, although none could identify a particular legal bias one way or another. The issue remains a mystery. Why would New Hampshire, generally considered the most conservative state in New England, have the highest proportion of government-run public libraries?

There is an interesting legal case in Vermont that illustrates the interesting hybrid nature of public libraries. In 2002 a dispute arose involving the West Hartford Library, operated by the town of Hartford. The town manager, operating on behalf of the Hartford select board, reduced the compensation of the library director after the board of trustees had given her a raise. The board felt the local government had usurped their authority under Vermont law and sued in Superior Court, which found for the town of Hartford. However, the board appealed to Vermont Supreme Court, which overturned the lower court ruling. The justices found that the legislature intended, through the enabling legislation, to give library boards complete authority to manage a public library's affairs, including all personnel and budgetary decisions over resources which include, but are not limited to, those allocated by the town. The court wrote in its opinion the following, "To the extent that a municipal library can be considered a department of the town, it certainly is not a department over which the town manager has been given direct control. The Board is directly accountable to the voters of the Town of Hartford."

It should be noted that Vermont law concerning public libraries provides the local option of the appointment of trustees by town officials, but this was not the instance in Hartford. In such a case, however, the court indicated the town of Hartford would have much more "direct control." It is also unclear if other states in New England make a similar distinction, but in general public library trustees have autonomy similar to locally elected school boards. One can debate whether the board of the West Hartford Library is more a governmental or civil society body, but in Vermont all public libraries clearly have civil society features whether designated an NGO or municipal.

Civil society is a sociological and increasingly political topic that, in this day and age, is unusual in that both the political right and left seem to agree on its importance to the health of democracy in America. The two perspectives differ to certain degrees, however, on why civil society is important and what can or should be done to strengthen it. Not coincidentally, admiration for and support for public libraries cuts across all American political stripes and demographics. Libraries are about as well regarded as apple pie, and particularly so in New England where civil society, social capital, and public libraries generally thrive.

Robert Putnam's pioneering work on civil society and social capital pointed out the decline of both beginning in the 1960s. His mapping of social capital levels in *Bowling Alone* provide a proxy for civil society engagement, even if there were and still are no numbers of NGO/civil society organizations (CSOs) in each state. As Putnam and others point out, civil society institutions are both difficult to define and count. A Cub Scout den is one, as is a town's American Legion post, but if counted, do these organizations have the same weight? In any event, imperfect as they are, measures of social capital (e.g., levels of interpersonal trust) will do since they are what's really important. CSOs are largely just the means to strengthen social capital and improve well-being, although one can't argue with the very real services many such organizations provide.

Current conservative public policy commentators and writers like Yuval Levin and Timothy P. Carney, in their respective books *The*

*Fractured Republic* and *Alienated America*, attribute the dire situations described in their titles in part to the trend Putnam identified two decades ago. More recent studies have confirmed Putnam's findings, although some indicate the fracturing of civil society may have lessened somewhat. Extensive data does support that public libraries in New England and elsewhere in America remain valued as key social institutions within their communities. What is significant, however, is this appears to be because they are increasing their role as a civil society community-connector, even as book circulation gradually declines. This is because the number of programs involving residents is increasing in number and scope. They are increasingly serving as community centers and, as such, they are the type of middle institutions whose loss many observers bemoan. Both the statistics collected annually by IMLS of public libraries across America and the New England case studies in this book document the trend.

Vermont has arguably the best state-wide public library system in America. Eighty percent of its facilities are located in rural areas, yet during 2016 the system offered over forty-eight programs per 1,000 people, up from forty-six the year before. Program attendance per 1,000 was an astonishing 740 people, meaning nearly three-quarters of the population attended a library program during 2016. In New England as a region the figure was 520, while the national average was 364 per 1,000. At the bottom of the IMLS statistics, the rate was under 225. As discussed in Section III, is it any wonder that Vermont tops the well-being (the best proxy available today for social capital levels) and opportunity indices national rankings, and the state in the Deep South with the library program attendance figure of 225 is at the rock bottom of both indices?

This data, while specific to public libraries, provides evidence of the type of correlation between weakened civil society and the social and economic "carnage" that Carney writes about in *Alienated America*. Where this book struggles, however, is moving past correlation—which is clear—to causation, which is not. Even Putnam, a researcher and scholar, had a difficult time pinning this down. Does the contraction of civil society cause alienation, or is it the other way around? Putnam identified a number of factors that appeared to have a negative effect on civic engagement, volunteerism, and other manifestations of civil society, none of which seemed to be overwhelming. Perhaps civil society's death is by a thousand cuts; or, to paraphrase Mark Twain, perhaps reports of its demise are greatly exaggerated.

The state-level IMLS data obviously obscures differences between communities within a state, but this is where the case studies contained in this book come in, both to offer a finer grain look and a more qualitative, if subjective, assessment. Several of the cases involve communities that could have appeared in Carney's book or other recent writing on the same topic, namely Turner's Falls, Athol, and Holyoke in Massachusetts, Norwich in Connecticut, Lisbon in New Hampshire, and Bridgton and Biddeford in Maine. All except Bridgton are former industrial towns or small cities that experienced the flight of manufacturing, and with it, well-paying jobs to the south or overseas. In these places, the wrenching changes started in the 1960s when civil society began its decline. Most have aging, if not ethnically diverse populations, although in terms of the second factor there are a couple of outliers. At least one case study location, Biddeford, appears today to be becoming more ethnically diverse, as the case study describes.

These communities share many characteristics, but no two are identical. Some have a surprisingly high mean household income, by which income inequality in the community obscures the households in distress. Norwich is an example of this, a community with the lowest well-being index ranking of any community measured in New England, yet with a mean household income of nearly $65,500. The case study community with the lowest mean household income is Bridgton, Maine, at $47,000, which from both the data and case study observation appears to have a low degree of income inequality (i.e., few households that are wealthy and few that are poor). In any event, the Bridgton Public Library, an NGO, is thriving with a strong cadre of user/supporters, a committed staff, and an engaged board of trustees.

Of the sixteen case studies, only three of the public libraries appear to be in any sort of distress. Two are in small former mill towns with the social problems that associate with that. Seeing either community in *Alienated America* would not be a surprise. Library usage appears anemic and the original Carnegie-era buildings have never been significantly expanded in size. The overall impression is a time warp. One would not be surprised to see a magazine issue from the 1970s in the periodical rack. Perhaps significantly, both are town libraries and the librarians and board members appear to lack drive and vision, in stark contrast with their counterparts interviewed in other communities. Tellingly, none of these libraries have a strategic plan for the future, which would have provided evidence of stronger community engagement. Presumably, the towns in which these libraries are located do not find them to be a high priority given other pressing needs. This is also presumably a reflection of the community's interest as well, as are the striking differences in state-level public library stats presented early.

If this hypothesis is correct—that public library health is tied in significant part to the vision and community engagement of its civil society leadership on the institution's board of trustees, and quite frequently, the local friends of the library nonprofit—what does this say about the prognosis for public libraries in communities with low levels of civic spirit, volunteerism, and social capital? The public library case studies provide clues since towns lacking these features are in many other ways no different socioeconomically than towns in which they are found, such as in Athol, Ashaway, and Bridgton. The elusive qualities that appear to be missing are strong local civil society (social capital) *and* governmental leadership.

# SECTION II

## New England Library Stories

THIS SECTION CONTAINS THE STORIES OF SIXTEEN PUBLIC LIBRARIES, in chronological order of their establishment. The criteria to select these case studies from across the six states in New England was purposeful. The first four are historic in that their establishment reflected firsts in New England or America as a whole. Some were selected because they are located in small cities that once had thrived based on their Industrial Age manufacturing. Others are located in rural areas or villages. Some are located in what are today well-endowed communities, while others are in locations that face challenges in terms of livelihoods, well-being, and social capital. Whatever the historic and current circumstances, they all have a story to tell and taken together help tell a collective story of public libraries in New England, and indeed throughout America, in the past, present, and future.

*Franklin Public Library* — Franklin, Massachusetts (1790)

*Scoville Memorial Library* — Salisbury, Connecticut (1803)

*Cary Memorial Library* — Lexington, Massachusetts (1827)

*Peterborough Town Library* — Peterborough, New Hampshire (1833)*

*Otis Library* — Norwich, Connecticut (1850)

*McArthur Public Library* — Biddeford, Maine (1863)

*Ashaway Free Library* — Ashaway, Rhode Island (1871)

*Holyoke Public Library* — Holyoke, Massachusetts (1886)

*Guilford Free Library* — Guilford, Vermont (1892)

*Bridgton Public Library* — Bridgton, Maine (1895)

*Kellogg-Hubbard Library* — Montpelier, Vermont (1896)

*Field Memorial Library* — Conway, Massachusetts (1901)

*Carnegie Public Library* — Turners Falls, Massachusetts (1903)*

*Athol Public Library* — Athol, Massachusetts (1914)*

*Lisbon Public Library* — Lisbon, New Hampshire (1926)

*Munson Memorial Library* — South Amherst, Massachusetts (1930)

*Carnegie library. For more about the Andrew Carnegie libraries see Appendix IV.

The public library vignettes span almost 150 years, beginning shortly after America gained its independence and running through the Gilded Age and Progressive Era. The latter was the height of the spread of public libraries from New England across the country, in large part due to the support of a single individual: Andrew Carnegie. But as the history of the earliest featured libraries shows, the beliefs and values that drove Carnegie were present a century earlier; he simply had the means to do on a national scale what others before him—at least in New England—had often done locally.

The libraries were selected based on a number of criteria including historic significance (especially, but not exclusively, the first four), interesting creation stories (e.g., Lisbon and Field Memorial), location within the townscape (e.g., Munson and Cary), and socioeconomic diversity (e.g., Bridgton, Holyoke, and Biddeford). All are located in villages, towns, or small cities, rather than larger cities in the region such as Boston, Hartford, or even Portland, Maine. This is because public libraries in America began in towns and the fact that in smaller localities they are more significant as anchoring social institutions simply because there are few other alternatives.

Each vignette starts by offering short history and a sense of place for the library location, followed by description of the physical setting within the townscape of the public library building. Next the case studies feature the particulars of current library use and future aspirations and plans. Photographs illustrate the text, highlighting specific features of each location; in the case of Franklin, which follows immediately, this includes the significance of the public library to the town's sense of identity.

Before moving into the vignettes, readers should reflect on the names of the public libraries covered. Many, but not all, mention "public." There are two "free" libraries, in Ashaway and Guilford. This designation was, of course, significant since the early libraries like Franklin's were technically public but not free of cost. Several are designated "memorial" to denote their benefactor or founder, including the Cary in Lexington and the Scoville in Salisbury. The McArthur in Biddeford, Kellogg-Hubbard in Montpelier, and Otis in Norwich are named after their benefactors, but without the "memorial" designation. The Kellogg-Hubbard and Otis library names give no sense that they are public at all, like the Redwood Library and Athenæum in Newport, Rhode Island, which was established and remains private to this day.

# Franklin Public Library

118 Main Street, Franklin, MA

Established: 1790 (book collection) and 1904 (library building)

Benefactor(s): Benjamin Franklin, Lydia Ray Pierce, and Annie Ray Thayer

The town of Franklin was incorporated in 1778 and is located in southeastern Massachusetts near the border with Rhode Island. Today it has a population of some 33,000 residents and a mean household income of approximately $123,200. The town area was first settled in the 1660s and was known as Exeter, but residents opted for the name change to Franklin at incorporation during the Revolutionary War in recognition of Benjamin Franklin's achievement in gaining French support for the nascent United States of America. It was the first town in America to be named after Benjamin Franklin.

The town's early economy and prosperity was based on agricultural production and later mill manufacturing. Franklin falls within the headwaters of Charles River watershed, which empties into Boston Harbor, but it is also located close to America's first industrial location established during the 1790s in northern Rhode Island on the Blackstone River, which flows from central Massachusetts through Providence into Narragansett Bay.

Location of the first public library in America (1790), Franklin, Massachusetts.

Horace Mann, born in 1796, may be Franklin's most famous native son; many scholars consider him the father of America's system of public education. Franklin is the home of Dean College, founded in 1865, a private residential college with some 1,200 students. Franklin also is the home of the "Red Brick School," one of the oldest one-room schoolhouses still standing in America, established some 185 years ago. Franklin's main claim to fame is, however, its public library, established in 1790, the first in America—and the world.

**Library History:** In 1785 the town fathers, including the Reverend Nathaniel Emmons of the Second Congregational Church, wrote to Benjamin Franklin reminding him of the honor bestowed upon him seven years earlier and requested that he acknowledge the act by donating a bell to grace the steeple of their planned town meeting house. Franklin responded that he would recognize the town with a donation of books, noting that "sense being preferable to sound." He subsequently had a colleague select an assortment of books in London. The collection of 116 volumes arrived in the town in mid-1786. By the next year, however, a controversy emerged over who should be allowed to use the books: only the members of church parish or any town resident. In 1788 five residents actually wrote to Franklin asking for him to clarify his intent with the donation. It is not known if he ever replied, but regardless, in June 1789 the town meeting voted to direct Reverend Emmons, who had the collection in his possession at the parish house, to lend books to inhabitants of the town at large.

In spite of this directive, Emmons refused, arguing that the parish library had existed for at least thirty years before the new donation from Franklin and that the new books should be merged with the existing collection and managed as it historically had been done. The town meeting, in a vote on Christmas Eve of 1790, decided the two collections should be handled separately and that the Franklin collection would henceforth be available to the general public.

Some participants suggested during this meeting that the town should add to the Franklin collection using taxpayer funds, but the group doubted "whether the town, without the aid of the General Court, can vote a Legal Tax to raise money for the purpose of additional books." Arthur W. Peirce recorded this information in the book *History of the Town of Franklin*; Peirce was the Headmaster of the (then) Dean Academy and husband of Lydia Ray, one of the donors of the 1904

The original books given to the town by Benjamin Franklin on public display.

library building discussed below. Significantly, Peirce notes that this discussion was the first instance known of a town meeting anywhere in New England considering the use of tax funding of a public library. This discussion predates the use of tax funding for the public library in Salisbury, Connecticut, by twenty years and of the library in Lexington, Massachusetts, by thirty-seven years. During this early period the Franklin Public Library collection was kept at the home of Reverend Emmons while he was minister of the Second Church (1773–1827).[20]

Horace Mann was born six years after the library was established and made use of it to discover the Classical world while growing up in Franklin before he departed to attend Brown University; his biography cites his reading of the five volumes of Thomas Gordon's *Tacitus*, part of the original collection donated by Franklin. His father, Thomas, was the library treasurer between 1802 and 1806. Mann became the Secretary of the Massachusetts Board of Education, and in the 1839 Third Annual Report he wrote that public libraries are necessary "adjuncts to public schools... for with no books to read the power of reading will be useless..." In the report he proposed the "establishment of a free circulating library in every school district of the state." Mann later supported the 1851 legislation in Massachusetts which permitted local jurisdictions to support public libraries through taxation.

This amounted to a call for a state-wide public library system at a time when only a very few scattered towns throughout New England had established the community institution. One can only speculate whether Horace Mann would have become the education visionary he proved to be had not the books at the Franklin public library been available to him. What is certain is that he valued reading, books, and libraries. Mary Peabody, a biographer, quoted him as saying, "Had I the power, I would scatter libraries over the whole land, as the sower sows his wheat field."

In 1858 the Franklin Library Association was formed, primarily to improve the preservation of the portion of the collection that originated from Benjamin Franklin. The following year the town gave physical custody of the entire library to the association. While public, the library was not yet free. The association charged six cents per week per volume borrowed. Even with this fee, the association could not make a go of it and the book collection reverted to the town in 1871. The town meeting also voted to establish a board of trustees and for a sum of money to purchase additional books. The town made its expenditure for its library in 1872. In that year as well, the first association president passed away and left a small endowment ($250 per year) to help operate the library. More importantly, the association reorganized under a new Commonwealth of Massachusetts law that had been passed at their instigation. The law permitted a town to appropriate tax monies to a library corporation so long as the corporation permitted inhabitants of the town free access to and use of the library. The Franklin Public Library thus became a free library in 1851.[21] In 1849 New Hampshire had become the first state in America to pass such legislation, which permitted the Peterborough Town Library to become the first taxpayer funded, free, town-administered public library (which subsequently remained continuously open).

In 1875 the library collection relocated from the high school to the main building block (the Ray Block) in Franklin, located on Main Street and the home of the Franklin National Bank and the post office. The town covered operating expenses and the association purchased new books to grow the collection. These efforts were successful, and by 1891 the book collection required a larger space. The library moved in 1891 into a new and larger Ray Block on Dean Avenue, near the corner with Main Street. Late in the decade, the library added open book racks along with the first card catalogue. One of the Franklin Library Association directors, William F. Ray, suggested in a report to the town that "in the near future some son of our town ... may gladly furnish for our Public Library a permanent building."

Perhaps William Ray knew something others did not at the time,

The original Franklin Public Library building.

for six years later in October 1904 the Ray Memorial building was dedicated as the new and permanent home of the Franklin Public Library, a gift of Lydia Ray Peirce and Annie Ray Thayer to honor the memory of their parents, Joseph Gordon Ray and Emily Rockwood Ray. The Ray family had been one of the wealthiest families in Franklin for some generations. Joseph's father, Edgar Knapp Ray, was a prominent businessman and early industrialist. The Ray family owned a large and successful farm in Franklin and wool and cotton mills on the Blackstone River just across the border in Rhode Island and Connecticut, and they had established the street railroad system in Franklin and surrounding areas and founded the Franklin National Bank. The Ray family also established an endowment through the Ray Memorial Association to provide for the library building. This support lasted until 1982 when the Franklin Public Library became a town department.

**The Physical Setting:** The Ray Memorial Building that houses Franklin Public Library is situated on the corner of Main Street and School Street, so named because the building stands across from the former Dean Academy, now Dean College. One block to the east on Main Street is the town's original business district clustered around the intersection of Main and Central Streets. Up Main Street to the west is the historic Franklin Town Common, surrounded by large homes and the huge Saint Mary's Parish Church building at the northwestern corner. This parish is the largest Catholic congregation in the Archdiocese of Boston with some 15,000 members. The library is part of the Franklin Cultural District.

The library building is large and imposing. Henry Hammond Gallison, a former Franklin resident, designed the building and also painted the large interior murals that grace the largest space, the former "delivery room," where the catalogue was located, and books were checked out. Gallison, a noted landscape painter at the time, also painted murals in the entry foyer and staircase leading to the lower level of the building where a public lecture hall is located. A year earlier Gallison, who lived and painted in Europe for a period, was honored by the Italian government, which purchased one of his paintings for its National Museum—the first of any American artist. Another artist, Tommaso Juglaris, who had studied under Gallison, painted the murals in the reading room. He was an Italian citizen and did much of the work on canvas at his studio in Italy. The noted Massachusetts historian, Samuel Atkins Eliot II, wrote in 1906 that the murals at the Franklin were Gallison's "greatest monument to his genius."

The reading room of the Franklin public library. Many of the interior spaces of the original building are ornately decorated with murals and other artwork.

In 1916 former President Taft visited Dean Academy on the occasion of its fiftieth anniversary. Writing to his hosts after the event he noted, "I have never seen a town library equal to that of Franklin. It is a work of art." In fact, few public libraries built at the beginning of the twentieth century, and none in town with a then population of 5,000 residents, can compare in terms of both the monumental architecture and its interior artwork. The Ray family and the people of Franklin no doubt wanted to do justice to Benjamin Franklin's gift and the honor it bestowed on them for all time. In 1989, in time for the next year's one hundredth anniversary, the town spent over $3 million to restore and expand the building to its current 30,000 square feet size and configuration.

**Library Use Today:** Befitting its pedigree, the public library is today at the center of community life in Franklin. While there are many places in America named after Benjamin Franklin, there is only one town with the claim to having the first public library in America, started with books from him. It is no wonder that the old-fashioned road signs announcing arrival in Franklin proclaim this unique history, and the town's Wikipedia entry begins with this claim to fame.

The library has been a town department since the early 1980s. The library's board of directors provides input and ideas to the town administrator who oversees administration of the institution. The board consists of five members appointed by the administrator subject to ratification by the town council. The library director serves as an ex officio member. Members review and make recommendations concerning the library's annual budget and assist with staff recruitment and selection. The five current board members and two associate members are all women.

There is also a Friends of the Franklin Library all-volunteer nonprofit, incorporated in 1992. The organization includes fundraising, outreach, programs, and memberships committees. The Friends encourage public support of the library and helps to raise supplementary financial support for programs and concerts for all ages, a summer reading program, book discussions, educational materials, and furnishings such a tables and chairs for the main reading room. In addition, there is an active teen advisory board.

Franklin is a family town with demographics which haven't changed much in recent decades. Many professionals reside in Franklin and job changes result in a relatively high number of transient households. Library patronage reflects the town makeup with perhaps 60 percent of users being children under 12, with teens and young adults another 15 percent each. Adults and seniors make up the balance. Franklin has a popular senior center that offers programs, some of which are in collaboration with the library. The library also collaborates on programming with Dean College, which draws patrons who live in the town only temporarily. The number of elderly in the town is average for the greater Boston area, and the library provides a shuttle for seniors and services to the homebound and those residing in the town's three nursing homes.

The annual budget is approximately $1.1 million and comes entirely from the town. There are eight full-time and seven part-time staff, a number of senior citizen volunteers who are able to write-off their donated time on taxes, sixteen regular volunteers, and a dozen teen volunteers. The staff oversee a thriving community institution led by library director, Dr. Felicia Oti, who holds a PhD in information science from the University of Michigan, Ann Arbor. All 33,000 citizens of the town are patrons and today use the Franklin Public Library more than ever. In 2019 total library visits numbered over 182,000, with wifi daily use averaging 650 discrete log-ons. Aside from checking out books or other items, some patrons visit the library to access the town's historic archives or research genealogy, or use the varied meeting, study, and reading rooms—one of the meeting spaces is for youth. Generous operating hours of between 60 and 63.5 hours per week, including Sunday afternoons during the non-summer months, foster the library's patronage.

Between 2018 and 2019 circulation topped 331,000 items, a 47 percent increase. This figure includes the physical and digital collections, items from the library of things (which includes games, appliances, and musical instruments), and items retrieved from other public libraries across the Commonwealth of Massachusetts through the Minuteman Library Network. Over the same two-year period use of meeting and study rooms increased by 112 percent, to nearly 2,200 reserved uses. The number of children's, teen, and adult programs increased 68 percent to nearly 490, with a 374 percent increase in teen programs alone. Not surprising, "tween" and teen participation increased 264 percent to nearly 1,500 individuals. Participation on all programs grew by 38 percent. Popular programs include: for Toddlers & 5+ (focused on social skills and early literacy)—Get Ready for Kindergarten, Construction Junction, and Local Hero Storytime; for tweens/teens (focused on leadership and confidence)—Girls Who Code, Chess Club, and Artist Amigos; and for Adults (focused on information and lifelong learning)—IT help desk, genealogy, and employment workshops.

The Franklin Public Library is particularly dedicated to community engagement with citizens and other local organizations. While many libraries conduct a survey of community members when preparing a new multiyear strategic plan, the Franklin conducts annual user surveys. Questions include reasons for the library use, most and least favorite things, and areas for improvement, including the addition of new services. In a recent survey, books and programs tied as the most important draw. Favorite things included the emphasis on local staff and the library's staff, while least favorite were lack of parking and summer hours that do not include Sundays. Engagement with other local organizations includes the Franklin Historic Society, more than twenty local book clubs, the senior center, educational institutions (particularly the Missile School and Dean College), and even the local farmer's market where people can check out books.

**The Future:** The Franklin Public Library has had three multiyear strategic plans to guide its service delivery in recent years and now is a year into a fourth plan. Building on very strong community support, the vision is basically to continue to sustain and grow a local institution that promotes lifelong learning and builds community. The library may be reaching a point where demand for its services cannot be fully addressed without further physical space (both interior and parking) and staff. The library director feels additional staff are especially important for increased community outreach (such as to day care centers where many of the town's young children spend hours each day while their parents work), and more pop-ups at community events (which are currently limited to the farmer's market).

Like a number of other public libraries featured in the book the location of the building, while prominent in the townscape, provides limitations on physical expansion. Located on a corner lot on Main Street with a Dean College building next door to the east, the only room for expansion is to the south. The parking lot could become building space, but that would acerbate the shortage of parking unless the library added expensive underground parking to the new library wing. Alternatively, the library could purchase the residence on the other side of the lot if and when it came onto the market. In the interim, the library may need to expand its offsite program offerings.

## Scoville Memorial Library

38 Main Street, Salisbury, CT

Established: 1803 (book collection) and 1894 (library building)

Benefactors: Caleb Bingham; Jonathan and Nathaniel Scoville

Salisbury is a small rural town in the far northwest corner of Connecticut. It was founded in 1741, first by Dutch settlers, and today has a population of approximately 3,700 and a mean household income of just over $103,000. In addition to farming, the early economy was based on local iron deposits, which established the area as a seat of an important iron industry from the pre-Revolutionary War era until the early twentieth century. The town provided cast iron to Connecticut's nineteenth century small arms industry, including Colt's Patent Firearms, and also for railroad car wheels. Salisbury lies at the southern tip of the Berkshire Mountains and the town contains the highest point in the state. The Housatonic River forms the eastern town boundary, but it is not navigable and since there are no falls mill industries never developed. Salisbury contains two well-known boarding schools, Hotchkiss and Salisbury School, founded in 1891 and 1901, respectively. Salisbury has the oldest Methodist church in New England, founded in 1789, and had the first public free library in America supported by local taxpayers, although it did not remain continuously open.

**Library History:** Salisbury's first library was founded in 1771 by Richard Smith who imported 200 books from London. Thirty-nine people contributed funds towards the cost and the Smith Library was born. The original subscribers established regulations for the library and noted in the preamble the reasons for establishing the Library: "Whereas, we the subscribers looking upon it consistent with our duty to promote and encourage every rational Plan that may be proposed for the Encouragement of true religion; for the Promoting of Virtue, Education and Learning; for the Discouragement of Vice and immorality ... a library of Books on Divinity, Philosophy and History &c may be conductive to bring to pass the above laudable design." In 1827 the Smith Library Company voted to broaden access to its collection to any town resident willing to pay an annual subscription fee of $3.34.

Another public library had been established in 1803 by Caleb Bingham with a donation of 150 books that were first placed in the minister's residence and later the town hall. A Salisbury native, Bingham was a book publisher and later became a trustee of the Boston Public Library. In 1810 the town meeting voted to require the selectmen to expend funds (one hundred dollars) for the purchase of books for the Bingham Library for Youth. The town meeting supported the library again in 1821, 1826, and 1836. During the middle of the century, however, the Smith and Bingham libraries languished and, in fact, were closed for a period with the books in storage. Fortunately, this state of affairs did not last long and in the 1880s the Salisbury Library Association was formed, and the library collection was returned to the town hall with a catalogue published in 1889.

The association's book collection, comprised of the former Smith and Bingham libraries, remained in the town hall until the final decade of the century. In the early 1890s, Johnathan Scoville, another successful native son, left $12,000 in his will for the purpose of constructing a distinguished library building, and the Scoville Memorial Library opened in 1894. Jonathan Scoville was born on a farm in the town, which besides agriculture also manufactured pig iron from ore mined on the property. Scoville attended Harvard and after graduation established with his brother, Nathaniel Church Scoville, a railroad car wheel manufacturing plant in Buffalo, New York, which ultimately made the family a fortune. Jonathan served as the mayor of Buffalo and as a United States Congressman. Nathaniel's family matched Jonathan's donation for the library construction, and in 1902 established an endowment, which continues support until this day. The Scoville family also provided funding for construction of the Salisbury Town Hall.

The original Scoville Memorial Library Building, circa 1894. The structure is in the National Register of Historic Places.

As an aside, after Nathaniel Scoville's death in 1890 at age fifty-eight, has widow, Frances, and six children moved to Fifth Avenue in New York City, and later they resided in the "World's Richest Apartment Building" at 741 Park Avenue. Frances traced her ancestry back to the *Mayflower* and the founder of Plymouth, Massachusetts. One of their two daughters, Edith, became a member of the National Society of the Colonial Grand Dames in 1943. Edith Scoville left Salisbury a beloved nature reserve on the outskirts of the town's main village.

Besides providing space for books, the Scoville Memorial Library building was designed to serve as a community center, and it contains a public auditorium, stage, and balcony for musical recitals and performances. A downstairs kitchen and pantry provide refreshments. The town was named after the famous city in England and a fifteenth century stone carving was donated by the Salisbury Cathedral, in England, and was placed over the fireplace in the main reading room, where it remains today. The Romanesque structure was placed in the National Register of Historic Places in 1982 based on an approved nomination form that cites the claim of first public support of a library, which it notes is based on historical research. The nomination states the following, "In 1978 Robert C. Hilton, writing in the *Library Journal*, endorsed the Salisbury claim, 'At Salisbury, Connecticut the first known municipal library taxation came about in 1810 as a result of the philanthropy of native son and Boston bookseller and publisher Caleb Bingham.'"

This portion of Litchfield County, Connecticut, has another early public library located in the adjacent town of Sharon. In this case the benefactor of the library, completed in 1893, was Maria Bissell Hotchkiss, the widow of Benjamin Berkeley Hotchkiss who made the family fortune from the local manufacture of tools (including the first monkey wrench) and then armaments, first in Hartford for Colt Remington and later in France where he developed the Hotchkiss gun, a revolving barrel machine gun used in WWI. Upon his death, Maria Hotchkiss became one of the wealthiest women in the Northeast and founded and endowed the Hotchkiss school, ensuring that worthy students from the area would not be charged tuition. The library's noted architect, Bruce Price, who designed many buildings on the Yale University campus, was the father of Emily Post, a socialite and author famous for writing about etiquette.

**The Physical Setting:** The Scoville Memorial Library is located on the prominent corner of Library and Main Street (Route 44) across from the main church in the village and the town hall, and down the street from the town common, which contains a Civil War memorial. Architecturally, the library is arguably the most distinguished building in Salisbury. The original structure was enlarged in 1981 through a well-executed addition to add space for additional book stacks, offices, and community events.

**Library Use Today:** A nongovernmental organization (NGO), governed by a board of trustees, operates the Scoville Library and is largely funded by private donations. Approximately 40 percent of the annual budget comes from the town of Salisbury, with the remainder evenly split between private donations (recently in the range of 450 benefactors) and the library's endowment. The town supports two local NGOs, one being the library, on a regular basis and its allocation to the Scoville

Interior view showing part of the original building's main hall.

has increased in recent years. The library has a staff of eight, all of whom work part-time except the director. There is a local friends of the library voluntary association that provides some funding and occasional volunteers for special projects. Both the town government and community residents strongly support the library.

The library contains over 30,000 items, including books from the original Salisbury Library Association collection as well as an archival collection containing historical items pertaining to the town's various villages. There are two meeting spaces available for use by community organizations or small groups. Monthly use ranges between 3,500 and 5,000 patrons, with greater usage in summer and on weekends given the town's popularity as a second home location. For this reason, unlike most public libraries, the Scoville is open both Saturday and Sunday. Salisbury has an older population, which is itself aging as lifespans increase. Fully 70 percent of patrons are adults, approximately half of which are over 65 years of age. Among the latter group, book checkout is the most frequent library use. Around 10 percent of users are children under 12. Teenage use is limited as they utilize school and other nonlibrary community resources.

The library provides the community with a number of programs including weekly children's story times, book clubs, meditation classes, and vintage movies. In the tradition of the lyceum, the Scoville hosts the Salisbury Forum, a series of four to five talks per year featuring an exchange of ideas and information with nationally known speakers. In addition, the library cohosts another speaker series with local businesses, the White Hart Inn and Oblong Books & Music. Susan Orlean, author of *The Orchid Thief* and *The Library Book*, was a speaker on the second book at a fundraiser for the Scoville. For a number of community programs, the Scoville also collaborates extensively with the Salisbury Association, which since 1902 has served as a civil society–based historical society, a cultural event organizer, and natural resource protector through a land trust.

**The Future:** The leadership of the Scoville have no plans for future physical expansion or major renovation work, as they feel they are currently serving their community well. They see opportunities for greater patronage through increasing awareness of existing library resources and adding programs to meet emerging community needs. Two examples are further supporting the increase in local entrepreneurship and better serving the aging population in the area.

## Cary Memorial Library

1874 Massachusetts Avenue, Lexington, MA

Established: 1827 (book collection) and 1869 (library building)

Benefactors: town meeting members; Maria Hastings Cary,
William A. Tower

Lexington, Massachusetts, lies in the northwest outskirts of Boston and was incorporated in 1713. Today it has a population of 33,000 residents and is one of the wealthiest communities in America with a mean household income of nearly $190,000. Lexington is renowned for being the site of the first shots in the Revolutionary War, which occurred on the town common April 19, 1775. Some 700 British "Regulars" marched from Boston with the objective of capturing arms and supplies in Concord, just west of Lexington. Having been warned during the middle of the night of the advancing British troops by Paul Revere, some eighty Lexington militiamen assembled in formation on the town common as the British troops arrived from the east at daybreak. Up to one hundred spectators watched from the side of the road. The militia did not attempt to block the road to Concord. A British officer demanded the militia disperse and may have also ordered them to "lay down your arms." The militia leader, Captain John Parker, told his men to disperse and return to their homes. They began to drift away, still with their arms, while the British commanders told their men to hold fire.

What happened next is not clear. One or two shots were fired, by which side will never be established with certainty. The massed British troops fired a massive volley of shots and followed with a bayonet charge. Eight militiamen were mortally wounded. Only one Regular was wounded and as the militiamen scattered, some of the Regulars continued on to Concord where the force split up to secure and search the town. A militia force of 400 confronted less than 100 British troops at the famous North Bridge. This time there is little question that the outnumbered British troops fired first. The shots that followed killed and wounded on both sides, but the British fled back to the center of Concord. During the afternoon while marching back to Boston through Lexington, the colonial minutemen hiding along the route harassed the Regulars. All told, British killed and wounded totaled nearly 250 men, while the comparable Patriot figure was less than 100. The Lexington and Concord battles on April 19 were a strategic American victory and marked the beginning of the Revolutionary War.

During the first half of the nineteenth century, Lexington continued as an agricultural community, supplying the growing nearby market of Boston. A railway first linked the town and city in 1846. During the latter half of the twentieth century Lexington's size grew rapidly, especially between 1950 and 1970 during which time the population almost doubled and became more commercially diversified. The town is located on the edge of the high-tech Route 128 corridor that boomed during this period, decades before Silicon Valley, due to the Cold War and the area's wealth of scientists and engineers—many graduates from Boston area colleges and universities. Since 1951, Lexington has been the home of MIT's Lincoln Laboratory located at Hanscom Air Force Base, one of the Department of Defense's premier research and development centers. Lexington's population is very well-educated and besides high-tech workers includes many professors from higher-education institutions in Boston and Cambridge, including three winners of the Nobel Prize in Economics. Examples of such residents have included Tim Berners-Lee, Noam Chomsky, John M. Deutch, Henry Louis Gates, Jr., Joseph Nye, and Robert Putnam. Lexington and Concord have also been linked with the development of New England Universalism and the Transcendentalism movement, led in the mid-1800s by Concord resident Ralph Waldo Emerson, who was also a major participant in the budding lyceum movement at the time.

**Library History:** The history of the public library in Lexington is interesting and a bit unique from others featured in the book in that establishment of today's public library, the Cary Memorial, took almost eighty years and thus was a multigenerational effort. As early as 1827 the town meeting voted to establish a juvenile library and to raise sixty dollars, by a tax, to purchase books.[22] Although the library passed out of existence in 1839, this appears to make Lexington the site of the oldest tax-supported public library in Massachusetts, and second community nationally to only Salisbury, Connecticut, whose town meeting established its public library as tax-funded in 1810.

During the 1830s two separate members-only library associations were also established, including one to benefit farmers and their families. The two associations later merged, and in 1862 the Farmer's Club was authorized to take charge of the collection, which was housed in a private residence.

In 1867 twelve citizens formed the Lexington Library Association, and this group apparently provided the impetus to another Lexington citizen, Maria Hastings Cary, to step forward the next year with an offer of $1,000 for additional books—if the town established a free public library and matched her donation. She asked the town to pledge an annual allocation thereafter of forty dollars for additional books and, importantly, to maintain and keep open without charge a building to properly house the library collection. Maria Hastings was born in 1801 on a farm in Lexington. Both her father and grandfather had fought in the Battle of Lexington. Maria married a native son from a nearby farm, who by then had done well and lived in Boston.

On April 20, 1868—almost ninety-three years to the day after the famous battle—the town meeting agreed to the terms, provided that another party donated another $400 or its equivalent in books. The town meeting also began annual appropriations for support of the Cary Library, which have continued to this day. The Farmer's Club promptly stepped forward and contributed its 401-volume collection, valued at $575. As Cary stipulated in her gift, the library established a board of trustees consisting of selectmen, school committee members, and representatives of local settled ministers to oversee the use of the contributions and operations of the library. When it opened in January 1869, the Cary Memorial Library boasted a collection of some 1,200 books, including 300 volumes obtained through gift and purchase from the library association.

However, the collection still lacked its own home, as the library was located over a general store on Main Street. In 1870 Cary offered $20,000 towards the erection of a town hall, and when it was completed the following year, the library found its new home on the first floor of the building. This arrangement lasted until 1906. Maria Hastings Cary passed away in 1881, leaving the library another $5,000 towards unspecified use. In 1885, reports indicate a total collection of over 29,000 volumes or roughly eleven books per Lexington resident. (This was quite an endowment for the time. In 1925 the ratio had dropped to a still respectable 7.9 books per person. As a matter of comparison, today the Massachusetts public library system provides just over 4.5 books per resident of the commonwealth.)

In 1887, a successful local businessman, William A. Tower, offered to erect a dedicated library building if the town would provide a prominent site on Main Street (now Massachusetts Avenue). The town meeting accepted the offer and shortly thereafter the heir of the Cary estate, the Cary's foster daughter, Alice B. Cary, stepped forward with a donation of $10,000 for the purchase of a corner lot near the town common.

In 1888 a group including Alice B. Cary was able to have legislation passed by the commonwealth legislature to create a library

The original Cary Memorial Library building located on Massachusetts Avenue, Lexington's main street.

corporation to, with the assent of the town, take over control of the Cary Library funds, books, and other property then held by the original trustees. The corporation board would continue to include representatives of the town selectmen and school committee but exclude representation by the settled ministers. However, the board of trustees refused the transfer of library assets to the corporation, which then sued.

The Massachusetts Supreme Court considered the case, *Cary Library v. Edward P. Bliss & Others*, in 1890. In their decision the court noted that, "It is perhaps not of much consequence in the consideration of this case or in the practical management of the trust, whether the legal title to the fund, or to the library itself, was in the trustees or in the town." The court found, citing many cases from around the United States and even England, that Maria Hasting Cary's "scheme which relates to the management and control of the fund and of the library cannot be disregarded as unimportant." The Court denied the petition by the library corporation, citing long-held precedent in the establishment of public trusts such as the Cary Library, and thus the originally constituted board of trustees continues to this day.

In 1893 and 1894 Alice Cary purchased additional land adjacent to the lot, and a decade later, in 1905, the entire library building plot was given to the town of Lexington. The building, built and opened in 1906, is considered the gift of Alice Cary to her foster mother, Maria Hastings Cary, who had passed away twenty-five years earlier.

**Physical Setting:** The Cary Memorial Library is situated in a place of very high prominence not only within Lexington but all of America given the town's unique history. The first bloodshed of the country's war of independence occurred footsteps away from the spot. William Tower had indicated a particular location for his library building donation on the corner of Main and Clarke Streets at the southeast tip of, what is today, the Lexington Common National Historic Site, where the first shots rang out over a one hundred years before. Across from the main library entrance stands the Minuteman statue of Captain John Parker, who commanded the Lexington militia that April morn-

The library today, with the famous Minuteman statue on Lexington common in the foreground.

ing. Just across the southern portion of the common, also known as Battle Green, is a Revolutionary War museum in the former Buckman Tavern. Some contemporary accounts of regular British troops on the green that morning said a colonial onlooker hidden behind the corner of the tavern fired the first shot. What is known for certain is that Parker and his men had spent the night at the tavern in anticipation and emerged from the tavern when the British entered Lexington at daybreak. Across Clarke Street from the Cary is a small park that contains a replica of the Old Belfry, the original of which the townspeople placed on the site in 1761 but moved to the common in 1768 and was there seven years later to ring the alarm on the morning of April 19, 1775.

Aside from several historic churches that predate it, the Cary Library is the only public building located around the town common. Others, such as the post office, town hall, and the Isaac Harris Cary Memorial Building, all adjacent to each other, are located further east on Main Street (now Massachusetts Avenue). The town hall (torn down and replaced in 1928) was built through a donation by Maria Hastings Cary. The Memorial Building, today the home of the Lexington Symphony, was a gift from Maria Hastings Cary's brother-in-law, who was her husband's successful business partner. The library is also located a few-minutes' walk from the Lexington High School, helping to ensure its use by many students for afterschool reading, research, and study.

Local architect, Willard Dalrymple Brown, who graduated from the MIT School of Architecture in 1894, designed the Cary Memorial Library building. His work reflected a variety of influences in fashion at the time, the height of the Progressive Era, especially the architecture and design of the Arts and Crafts movement more common on the west coast of America. The design is quite eclectic and unlike other public libraries of the day, including the thousands of Carnegie libraries constructed across America. The use of fieldstone as a design element reflects the massive stone foundation of the nearby minuteman statue. The Cary Library's design may well have reflected not only the architect's aesthetic style but also the strong local influence of Transcendentalism.

**Library Use Today:** Reflecting the values and needs of the community in which it is located, the Cary Library is one of best endowed and used public libraries in Massachusetts—and indeed all of America—

The main space with stage to right.

population size. As a library trustee noted for Lexington, "they come for the schools and stay for the library." An official town welcoming committee meets all new Lexington residents and one item in the move-in package is a library card.

While the Cary Library is run today as a department of the town of Lexington, it is a fascinating example of the type of public-private partnership with hybrid governance found among public libraries in New England. The original board of trustees still exists to help administer the endowment, set policies, and influence major decisions such as the hiring of the library director. Since 1999 there has been a library foundation with a prime role of fundraising especially for periodic capital campaigns. There is also an active Friends of the Cary Library that oversees the book shop for fundraising, and supports programming such as library-wide summer reading. This 501(c)(3) nonprofit is a member of the Massachusetts Friends of Libraries, a networking and advocacy group that lobbies elected officials within the commonwealth for public library support.

The Asian American population in Lexington grew by 91.4 percent between 2000 and 2010 and has continued to expand as an overall proportion of the town's population since then. Of the school age population, this ethnic group constitutes nearly 30 percent. They are avid library users and supporters; however, Asian Americans could be better represented on the Cary Library's governing and support bodies. Library leaders encourage this with continuing outreach and engagement attempts.

The overall size of the board of library trustees today is approximately thirty-five people, with five members each from the town Select Board, School Committee, and churches. Each year the full board of trustees selects five members for the executive board, which works closely with the director. The executive board oversees the financial affairs and operational policy of the library and also selects the library director who reports to the board. However, the director's annual performance review is conducted by the town manager, with board input, as the role is technically a town employee. The current director is only the ninth in the Cary Library's 150-year history.

The annual budget appropriation from the town of Lexington is in the range of $2.8 million. This covers all staff costs, utilities, and building maintenance. The Cary Library Foundation contributes another $250,000 for programming costs, with the Friends of the Cary Library donating approximately $40,000 mainly for book purchase. Recent state aid has run $50,000 per year. Staffing is robust with thirty full-time equivalent positions. There are also fifteen full-time volunteers, and another fifty to sixty people volunteer two or three times a week. The director noted volunteerism across many civil society organizations in Lexington.

Over the past five years, library use has ranged between 525,000–550,000 patrons per year. In terms of circulation, the Cary Library is the sixth most widely used public library in Massachusetts and, aside from the public library in Montpelier, VT, has the highest use among the libraries featured in *Common Place*. Since the top five public libraries are located in larger towns and cities, including Boston, Cary Library's per capita patronage is the highest in the commonwealth and among all the *Common Place* case studies. Contrary to other case study libraries, patronage has slipped somewhat during the past five years, while circulation has increased. The use of quiet study rooms has grown during this period, while library Wi-Fi use surged from 16,456 patrons in 2014 to 305,880 in 2018.

The library's total holdings include over 312,000 items, of which 209,000 are books and other print materials. Total circulation in 2018 was just under 870,000 items. The Cary Library offered over 875 programs, which drew some 26,650 patrons. An example of a popular foundation-supported program is Library After Dark, which offers musical performances and lectures geared for the whole family between the hours of 7 and 9 p.m. The Cary Library prides itself on the commitment to accessibility, with numerous physical and program features in place. There is also a community-wide door-to-door book delivery service available.

In spite of the Cary Library's large pool of patronage, significant collections and programming, there are things it does not do. This is a matter of choice that closely reflects community needs. Lexington has a rather new community center that includes a senior center. Many public meetings once held at the Cary Library now meet at the center. Lexington also has a vibrant community education program outside the Cary Library that welcomes both young people and adults interested in lifelong learning. Likewise, much programming oriented at seniors is offered by the senior center and not the Cary Library. The demographics of library users reflect this; approximately 40 percent of users are below of the age of eighteen, with another large proportion between the ages of forty and sixty-five years of age. This patronage reflects the overall demographics of Lexington, which has a high proportion of households with school-age children. Although the library has a teen room, there is no makerspace lab or high-tech programming. The emphasis is on reading, study, and support for community service volunteering. This too reflects the interests of the community, which are a bit unique.

**The Future:** The Cary Library had a comprehensive Strategic Plan covering the period between 2014 and 2017, which at the direction of the board focused outward on community needs and interests. While the plan period has ended, this emphasis on community engagement continues while acknowledging the importance of the institution around the core area of literacy and reading and that the town possesses other centers for community activity.

The earlier planning effort noted that in the decade ending in 2020, the town's demographics will have shifted towards a larger proportion of residents between the ages of twenty-five and thirty-four and those over fifty years of age. The highest growth rate was projected to be within the sixty to seventy-four age group, at over 23 percent of the total population versus around 17 percent in 2010. As the plan noted, these changes would figure significantly in the library's collection development, programming, and other services, such as the door-to-door program.

The library does have an updated Strategic Plan as well as an Action Plan covering FY20–22 with projects across all library departments. An interesting example is to expand the library's experiential learning opportunities including the current library of things. The plan is to expand the number and types of hands-on activities to patrons of all ages, improving library spaces to make them more adaptable to participatory programming. The Cary Library will partner in some efforts with community organizations, such as Kids Cooking Green, that specialize in this type of programming. The library will also expand the library of things collection based in part on user suggestions. Current items in the collection range from birding kits (consisting of binoculars and guidebooks) to eyeglasses for people who are colorblind.

The Cary Library's strategic priorities, developed with significant public consultation during the planning process, will continue to guide the library in the foreseeable future. These include:

- the provision of books and information
- promotion of experiential learning through making and play
- further increasing accessibility for everyone
- promotion of human connections and dialogue
- visioning the future as vibrant as the past, including nontraditional uses

In terms of the first priority, the library director noted the future role of not just the Cary Library but all public libraries in assisting users to identify the most factual information obtainable, both from books in the collection and digital sources including the internet. She noted this is not an entirely new function, but that in the Information Age and era of "alternative facts" finding accurate information can be challenging. The library must undertake this in the unbiased and nonjudgemental manner that reference librarians have followed as long as libraries have existed.

## Peterborough Town Library

2 Concord Street, Peterborough, NH

Established: 1833

Benefactors: Reverend Abiel Abbot

Peterborough is a medium-sized town with a current population of about 6,300 in south-central New Hampshire along the banks of the Contoocook River, incorporated in 1760. Its mean household income is today nearly $73,000. Like many other New England settlements of that era, Peterborough became a prosperous mill town producing cotton and wool fabrics, paper, boots and shoes, baskets, and carriages. During the past sixty years Peterborough developed as a cultural center with a summer theatre, a popular folk music festival, and the MacDowell Colony, a creative retreat where Leonard Bernstein wrote *Mass*, Aaron Copland composed *Billy the Kid*, and Thornton Wilder wrote his Pulitzer-winning play, *Our Town*—which was based on Peterborough. The town has been called by *Byte* magazine "the per capita magazine production capital of the world" with over one hundred published there; many, like *Byte* itself, involving computers and technology. Given its small size and somewhat isolated location, Peterborough is today a startup hub with approximately one-third of town employees working as home-based entrepreneurs or telecommuters working for businesses around the United States and Europe. Brookstone, the formerly ubiquitous shopping mall store, was founded in the town in 1965, as was Eastern Mountain Sports (EMS). However, in spite of this remarkable history, Peterborough's true claim to fame may be its town library—the first continuously-open, tax-supported public library operated by a local government in the world.

**Library History:** The first library in Peterborough was a social library, a membership society established in the 1790s. In 1827 the Reverend Abiel Abbot was charged with heresy by the religious establishment in Connecticut and came to Peterborough to minister at the Unitarian

Church. Within a few years Abbot, a Harvard University graduate in 1787, led the establishment of the town's first preparatory school, the Monadnock Academy, established a juvenile library in his home, and organized the Peterborough Library Company, a dues-paying membership library. Based on this experience, Abbot put forward a proposal "that a portion ($750) of the State Literary Fund be used for the purchase of books to establish a library, free to all citizens of Peterborough," which was passed by the town meeting on April 9, 1833. The fund, established by the state legislature in 1821, was generated from a tax on capital stock of New Hampshire banks, but it was not adequate to build the planned state university according to the original intention.

Based on the Peterborough public library, in 1849 the New Hampshire state legislature became the first in the United States to pass a law authorizing towns to raise money to establish and maintain public libraries. A similar law was passed in England the following year and in neighboring Massachusetts in 1851. In 1965 the New Hampshire state legislature passed a resolution recognizing Abbot's role in founding the "first free library in the world supported by taxation." While there were other instances of local tax revenue being used to support a public library (see the earlier cases of the Scoville Memorial Library in Salisbury, Connecticut, and the Cary Memorial Library in Lexington, Massachusetts), his accomplishment warranted the acknowledgment since the Peterborough Town Library was supported by both taxation *and* was free to users.

Plaque on the wall of the original building commemorating the historic nature of the Peterborough Town Library.

The original library building's main entry.

The original collection comprised one hundred books and was housed in the town's main general store and post office. As the collection grew, the collection required additional space, and in 1873 the library relocated to the town hall. In just a few short years, the library needed additional space, and local citizens joined together to raise funds for land and construction of a dedicated library building. A citizen group purchased the land, and two former residents supplied the majority of the funds required for the construction—they were descendants of early settlers, then living in Illinois—with the condition that their cousin, a respected local engineer, be given charge of the building's design and construction.

The structure was built in 1893 on a prominent downtown corner and housed a collection of 6,000 volumes. The plain brick building, basically a shoebox, was functional and most importantly fireproof. The town meeting also established a (then) three-member board of trustees. The trust gave the town free use of the building, including a public reading room and space for storage of town records, provided that the town not tax the property, provide a "sufficient sum annually" to pay a librarian, heat and maintain the building, and keep the library open for town residents six hours per weekday and two hours on Sunday. Over the years, donations have augmented the town's support. These gifts ranged from $100 given by a native who moved to California, a $5,000 donation from Andrew Carnegie in 1901, and the establishment of a trust fund endowment in 1914 through the generosity of David F. McGilvray, whose business interests were split between Boston and Peterborough. Another benefactor gave a significant donation to the trust fund in 1957, the year of the library expansion.

**Physical Setting:** The town library is located on the most prominent corner in Peterborough, Main and Concord Streets, on what is now Route 202, a major pre-Interstate thoroughfare which stretches from Hartford, Connecticut, to Bangor, Maine. It is sited near the town hall, located across the river that flows through the town and once was the basis of the area's prosperity. The original main entrance is on the south side of the building on Main Street, although the later addition of car parking and more floor space shifted the main entry to the east side of the building on Concord Street.

Like many early libraries, this one was sited and designed for pedestrian use. With the advent of motor vehicles, the library required a parking area. The building expanded in 1957 and again in 1978, both with parking spaces added to the property—which is hemmed in on three sides. The latter expansion required acquiring an adjacent historic residential property, which was razed, but insufficient parking remained a problem. The library purchased the next property to the north, another historic house and barn, in 1998 through a large donation from a former library volunteer, but a public outcry met plans to again demolish the historic structures. The first special town meeting in twenty years convened to discuss the issue, and shortly before the event the parties reached a compromise to raze the barn for parking but save and restore the house. The library raised $50,000 for this purpose, and the Friends of the Peterborough Town Library opened the Keys-Sage House, owned by the trustees, as a seasonal bookstore.

The original library structure was plain, perhaps in part because it was designed by an engineer and not an architect. However, twenty years after it opened, the trustees added a colonnaded front portico at the Main Street entrance, topped with a bronze pineapple, the traditional symbol of New England hospitality. (Pineapples brought to the colonies on sailing ships from plantations in the Caribbean were in such high demand as an exotic luxury item denoting good taste and wealth people rented them out for use as decor at affairs and then later sold to those who could actually afford to eat them.)

Years later, in 2007, an artist affiliated with the MacDowell Colony was commissioned to paint a mural on the ceiling of the portico. The scene depicts the confluence of the local Contoocook and Nubanusit Rivers—both names given by the native Algonquin tribe that inhabited the area prior to the arrival of Europeans. The artwork reflects both the natural history of the area and special relationship between the library and MacDowell, but unfortunately few users today experience either the portico or mural as they enter the main building entrance from the parking lot on the north side of the building. The library has future plans, discussed below, to address this issue.

**Library Use Today:** The last available library use statistics, from 2016, indicate that the Peterborough Town Library had over 43,000 books, some 4,000 library card holders (64 percent of the town's population), 71,500 visitors (an average of 200 patrons per day), over 61,500 borrowed items, and another 7,000 downloaded ebooks. The library offered over sixty adult programs, and nearly 3,200 children attended programs. Programming includes book groups, story times, drop-in tech assistance, films and discussion, and assistance for genealogical research. The library recently started a "discussions we should and need to have but don't" workshop series designed to foster thoughtful and respectful conversations on important but sensitive topics such as racism, human rights, and teaching in the public-school system. Special programming for teens includes a teen advisory group, Lego league, book club, and help with homework and college admission exams.

The library has a full-time staff of six, all town employees, assisted by five regular volunteers. The 1833 Society (see below) and friends of the library have another forty active volunteers each. The board of trustees has five members elected by the town of Peterborough selectmen. The board selects and hires the library director, establishes all library policies, and oversees the town's library endowment. The 1833 Society has established a separate endowment related to the recent building expansion and renovation campaign.

For town residents, library cards are free and there are no fines for overdue books. Non-Peterborough residents can obtain cards for a small fee. Book circulation declined approximately 1 percent in 2017 but appears to have plateaued since then. Interestingly, the library director feels increased programming, such as the popular "Conversations About Race" book group, has boosted book circulation. In terms of patrons, the library sees heavy use by adults, particularly seniors who comprise around 80 percent of library users. The library does not offer service to homebound members, but shuttle buses make several trips a week from senior housing sites in the area.

The town of Peterborough is obligated to provide resources for all library annual operating expenses, including maintenance of the building which is owned by the town. Significantly, the annual library budget is separated out from other town departments and services and is directly voted upon by the town meeting. The town meeting also approved the building expansion and renovation campaign, and the three-million-dollar bond issued in support, both put before it by the town selectmen.

The board of trustees chairperson and library director characterize community support as very strong, on the part of both residents and elected officials. The existence of and strong participation in the Friends of the Peterborough Library and 1833 Society reflects the first, while financial and political support from the Town Select Board reflects the latter.

Peterborough resident Tyler Ward participated in a recent session of the library's "Difficult Discussion" program, a workshop series conducted by a local psychologist. Ward was attending because he thought the program would be helpful in his work as one of the town's three selectmen. Ward, a carpenter who is in his late-40s, has lived in the town for eight years and, for over half of this period, has served on the select board which in addition to many other responsibilities selects the five members of the library board of trustees. He also serves on the town's heritage commission and on the board of a makerspace nonprofit. With these volunteer civic duties, Ward is an example of why civil society is so strong in Peterborough. He characterized community support for the library as "very, very strong," noting the May 2018 standing-room only town meeting attended by some 650 residents who voted 80 percent in favor of the town issuing a three-million-dollar bond to support the library's expansion and renovation. He noted that typical town meeting participation rarely exceeds 200 people. Ward also mentioned that at the town's 2018 Veterans Day commemorations one of the speakers mentioned the value of the library to the area's veterans.

**The Future:** Perhaps not surprisingly given its unique history, the board of trustees, town managers, library staff, and many citizens of Peterborough have given an extraordinary amount of time and attention to the future of the town library. Although the library is a town department, a 501(c)(3) nonprofit, library trustees requested the formation of the 1833 Society, in 2011 to raise funds to finance a major library upgrade estimated to cost $8.5 million. By June 2021 over $5.5 million in private funds was raised which added to the $3 million bond passed by the town meeting, allowed ground to be broken in June 2020 for the expansion and restoration of the original building. This project razed the earlier additions, renovated the original library structure, and nearly doubled the floor area for books and programming. It also created a riverside terrace to better take advantage of this scenic natural resource. Due to experience with COVID, during construction UVC features were added to the HVAC upgrade.

As important as the physical expansion, improved functionality, and appearance of the new library are, equally important of course is what goes on inside. Here, too, stakeholders gave much thought. In early 2013 the Peterborough library trustees, 1833 Society, and the town, assisted by the University of New Hampshire Cooperative Extension, planned and conducted a community library visioning forum to gather citizen input on plans for the renovated and revitalized town library.

Participants identified the strengthens and weaknesses of the current library and then turned to envisioning the library in ten years. For the latter exercise, an "impact and feasibility matrix" facilitated identifying the six highest impact and most feasible improvements, which participants then identified their top three overall priorities using a poll. These were presented to the other groups, and the entire forum then voted on its top six vision items. These, in rank order, included: (1) flexibility and adaptability of space and resources to adapt to future needs; (2) a dynamic community center for lifelong learning and engagement opportunities for all ages; (3) aesthetics: look, feel, and layout of the new library; (4) building that is sustainable, high performance and flexible; (5) staff and services; and (6) building that is

The new expansion (left) adjoining the original building. For the first time, the library's riverside location is featured of with the addition of an outdoor plaza.

green and flexible, while preserving history of both place and books. A similar exercise conducted today, or in most any other community in America, would likely yield similar results.

Reflecting and building on the forum during the summer of 2015, the 1833 Society led a series of meetings involving library staff, library trustees, and 1833 members to establish guiding principles for the Library of the Future project, with an emphasis on community. An interior gallery will display the work of local artists and public art will adorn the new riverside outdoor social space, which will have a café to promote casual meetups with friends and colleagues. The riverside area on the downtown side of the building will foster increased pedestrian access to the library. Meeting rooms of different sizes will be available for a variety of groups ranging from one-on-one tutoring, to small business client consultations, to community forums. Meeting space will be available both during and after library hours.

In addition to the focus on the expansion and renovation of the physical structure, Peterborough is one of many public libraries across America that, over the past five years, has participated in and benefited from the Aspen Institute Dialogue on Public Libraries, supported by the Bill and Melinda Gates Foundation. The initiative issued a report in 2014 that contained "strategies for success" and "action steps for library leaders, policymakers and the community." The strategies and sub-elements within them all seem rather self-evident; e.g., "ensure long-term sustainability of public libraries," but the suggested action steps are more specific, and many were helpful to Peterborough in visioning and planning the library's future.

Out of the visioning forum, consideration of the Aspen Institute's suggested action steps, and over 700 town survey respondents came the Peterborough Town Library Strategic Plan 2017–2019, which contains interconnected vision and mission statements, as well as six key goals. Given their relevance to public libraries across New England and indeed America, these deserve highlighting. Together they will help to establish Peterborough as a best practice public library.

**Vision**—Support a community where all people are encouraged to explore new ideas, contribute to the community and have opportunities for success, growth and joy.

**Mission**—The Peterborough Town Library champions literacy and encourages life-long learning by providing resources that enrich, educate and entertain. We strengthen our community by promoting connections between people, ideas and knowledge.

**Goals**—Champion literacy in all forms; support community connections; strengthen visibility and usage of the library; develop and empower staff to excel in their work; maintain a committed and engaged Board; and support the 1833 Society in fulfilling our vision for a new and library for the future of Peterborough.

Notable is the championing of literacy "in all forms," which the strategic plan notes, include skills in media, finance, digital technology, health, civics, employment, and basic literacy for patrons of all ages. Also notable is that half of the plan's goals cover library staff, board of trustees members, and the key civil society organization, the 1833 Society, leading the library's current expansion, renovation, and revitalization.

For a public awareness and fundraising event in March 2018, the library trustees and 1833 Society invited noted Harvard political scientist Robert Putnam to speak on the topic of "Why state-of-the-art libraries are essential to building community and restoring American democracy." Putnam, who lives part-time in the nearby town of Jaffrey, talked about his work, the decline of social capital documented in his groundbreaking book, *Bowling Alone,* and how public libraries are a key means in helping to restore this essential, civil society–based resource. (This issue is discussed further in the final section of the book.)

When asked about anticipated library use in the next five- to ten-year period, the board of trustees chair, Marcia Patten, and library director, Corinne Chronopoulos, forecast a significant increase resulting from the building expansion and renovation, especially among seniors and involving nonbook community programming. Selectman

Tyler Ward agrees, adding the library has a role to play in providing even greater support to the town's many nonprofit organizations and contributing to the area's reputation as an incubation hub. He also sees the library as a center for lifelong learning oriented to the town's sizable and growing senior population.

The renovation and expansion work were completed in September 2021, on-time and on-budget in spite of the pandemic. During the fifteen-month construction period the entire library (materials and operations) was moved into nearby temporary quarters. In the month following reopening the library experienced over 10,000 patron visits including those by nearly 150 new card holders. Use of five new community meeting rooms was in particularly high demand. Examples of users include town civic groups, nonprofit boards, arts organizations and individuals working remotely. Library use by teens has doubled, including daily after-school groups that study and discuss topics such as sexual violence on campus.

## Otis Library

261 Main Street, Norwich, CT

Established: 1850

Benefactor: Joseph Otis

First settled in 1659 through a purchase of land from the Mohegan Native American tribe, the city of Norwich was incorporated in 1784, one of the first five Connecticut cities. The population today is approximately 40,500 and the mean household income is nearly $65,500. Norwich was the birthplace of Benedict Arnold, perhaps the most famous traitor in American history, but on the other hand, during the American Revolution the city supported the Patriot effort by providing ships loaded with munitions that became renowned for eluding British warships.

The abundant waterpower available on the Yantic and Shetucket Rivers, which join at the city and then form the Thames River flowing south to Long Island Sound, provided the motive power for textile factories, which dominated the local economy by the mid-1800s. Norwich prospered and reaped the added benefits of well-established rail connections north, linking industrial areas of central and western Massachusetts with the port of New London on the sound. For a period, it was one of the largest cities in the Colonies. Norwich became a well-used stop on the Underground Railroad and attracted many freed slaves after the Civil War with the prospect of employment in the thriving mills.

Today, the Mohegan Sun and Foxwood Resort casinos are not far from Norwich, both on Native American lands. The first resort employs some 10,000 workers including many Norwich residents, albeit in mainly low-wage jobs. In spite of employment opportunities, residents of Norwich and surrounding towns complain about the impacts of the casinos on traffic and costs for housing and some local services.

In spite of its rich and at times prosperous history, today southeastern Connecticut includes some of the most distressed communities in New England. Norwich has experienced a decades-long decline that has only recently shown signs of ending, and as of 2021 the city is considered by state officials as Connecticut's second most distressed municipality.

Indeed, Norwich was selected for the public library sample precisely for this reason. Of all the communities in New England included in the 2017 Gallup-Sharecare Well-Being Index discussed in Section III, Norwich–New London places last, in 151st place among the 186 communities across America. This is in spite of the fact that in terms of its financial ranking the area falls above the mean in 77th place. A very low purpose score placing it in 181st place and a community ranking of 161st pulled down its overall score.[23] The next section discusses the place of the Otis Library in such an environment and the steps it is taking to address community well-being.

**Library History:** Joseph Otis founded Otis Library in 1850. He was born in Yantic, Connecticut, a village on the outskirts of Norwich. He left the area when he was twenty-one and prospered as a businessman

The original Otis Library built in 1850 in the foreground. The small structure to the left is the annex added in 1892.

first in Charleston, South Carolina, and later in New York City. Otis returned to Norwich in 1838 at age seventy, and a decade later, he purchased books and land on a prime corner in the center of downtown directly in front of city hall to construct a public library. The cost of the land and building, a two-story structure that took the form of a large house, was $10,500. The library opened in 1850 in the lower floor, while upstairs was a study for the pastor of the nearby church (see below).

Norwich actually had a series of circulating libraries since 1793, the first two of which were open to the public through subscription. The Norwich Library Association was established in 1796 but was dissolved in 1843 due to "public indifference." However, the Norwich Mechanics & Manufacturers Library began in 1835 among a select group of subscribers but was later open to the general public. The annual subscription was two dollars. It appears the association merged its collection with this library, so when Otis Library opened, with a dedicated building no less, it filled a community void.

Otis handpicked the founding board of trustees that would operate the Otis Library. The four members included the pastor of the Second Congregational Church, the city's largest denomination located across the street from the library; the former mayor, Governor of Connecticut, and United States Senator; the president of the Norwich Bank and Director of the Norwich & Worcester Railroad; and a local physician. It is important to note that the Otis was not originally a free library; citizens had to pay for a subscription, which cost one dollar per year in 1865.

When he passed away four years later, Otis left $6,500 in his will to endow the library operations as overseen by the trustees. The Otis Library is the city of Norwich's public library, and while the city has historically been and remains the single largest financial contributor to the library, the Otis remains an independent entity overseen by a library association and has never been a municipal department. While the civil society roots of the public library are not unusual, the fact that Otis has remained a nongovernmental organization for its entire

170-year history is, given Norwich's earlier prominence and prosperity. This was a matter of choice, which is also reflected by the McArthur Public Library in Biddeford, Maine, and the Holyoke Public Library, which have similar histories as nongovernmental organizations.

The Otis Library nearly closed in 1870, again due lack of public support, which resulted in a debt of $1,500. The year before the board of trustees voted to ask two of its members to investigate the "provisions of law for a Town Tax to support a public library." In short order they reported back that it would "not be advisable to pursue the tax and the matter was dropped" (Jenkins, 17). It was also around this time that the close relationship between the library and the Norwich Free Academy (NFA), a prominent local private school, was established which continues to this day. The Otis board reserved a seat for the NFA principal or his/her representative. By the end of the decade the Otis's fortunes rebounded with a significant bequest of some $15,000.

In 1891 the board voted to make Otis a free library, provided $1,000 could be raised first. One of the trustees made the contribution and volunteered to match the amount through new subscriptions for a final year before free use began. This trustee, and another who was also a successful local manufacturer, then offered to contribute $7,500 if another $10,000 could be raised during the final subscription drive. The fundraising campaign was successful, and subscriptions jumped from 470 to over 1,400 in just a month! The board also voted to extend use privileges to residents of contiguous towns.

The Connecticut General Assembly enacted legislation in February 1893 enabling towns to support public libraries through taxation. The board acted quickly and put before a special session of the town meeting at the end of May a resolution of support. Included in the deal was that the board of selectmen could nominate a Norwich representative to the board of trustees. The town meeting adopted the resolution by acclamation and made the first appropriation for $3,000 in October of that year and named a judge to the trustees. The next year another large bequest was made to the Otis, this time from a wealthy farmer. His obituary reported that, "Though possessing only a common school education, he had a fondness for study and passed all his spare hours in the company of good books" (Jenkins, 42).

In 1897 the Otis opened a de facto branch library, which illustrates its community engagement and concern for the disadvantaged that continued throughout its history. In the nearby village of Falls Mills a "university settlement" had been established, part of the settlement house reform movement begun the year before in New York City's Lower East Side. Settlements were intended as an alternative to public charity and provided advice, assistance, and education to the poor and new immigrants. Library records note that of the 250 books initially lent to the university settlement, 17 percent were written in French, illustrating a demand from young mill workers from French Canada.

In 1919 the board heard a suggestion by a town resident to add a children's librarian, but it would be another thirty-five years before the Otis Library opened its children's library. In the interim, the library added a children's room in 1927 as a result of major renovations and alterations to the library's interior. During the height of the Depression, the library implemented an interesting experiment in which books for young people were transported to a number of local playgrounds where they were read in situ during a story hour and checked out by cardholders. In 1954 the children's library moved to the nearby Olcott House, purchased and renovated at a cost of approximately $15,000. Local school children moved the books to the new facility, some using toy wagons.

By the beginning of the 1960s the lack of space in the original Otis building and inability to expand to adjoining properties left the board with no option but to seek a new site to allow the Otis to function as a modern public library. The board considered a number of options before opting to move into the space of a former department store located in a downtown building on Main Street owned by the state of Connecticut. The building cost was $425,000, and after selling the Otis property and children's library, the new library opened in August 1962. In later years the city of Norwich purchased the original Otis building to serve as an annex to the city hall across the street.

The Otis Library relocated in 1962 to the former Enterprise department store building located on Main Street in the heart of downtown.

Recently the lower floor of the building became a stylish coffee house.

**Physical Setting:** As noted above, from 1850 to 1962 the Otis was in a brick Greek Revival structure across from city hall in Union Square in the heart of the historic downtown district. In 1892, a new annex provided short-lived relief from overcrowding. However, before the early decades of the twentieth century had passed, overcrowding once again became severe. With no room for expansion in the Union Square facility, the children's library moved to an off-site location to free space for the library's ever-growing collections and ever-increasing number of patrons.

By the late 1950s, it became clear that more drastic measures were necessary to accommodate the Otis collections and provide adequate services to the area's population. In the 1960s the library moved to its new home on Main Street, a previous department store which had decamped to the growing suburbs. By the early twenty-first century, the library was again straining to accommodate the needs of its patrons and a growing immigrant population employed at the two Native

American casinos located nearby. In 2007, as part of a downtown revitalization initiative, an $8.4 million renovation and expansion doubled the physical space of the library to 40,000 square feet. Otis Library today resides on Main Street on the edge of downtown, alongside the Shetucket River, a short walk from its original home in Norwich's historic district.

**Library Use Today:** While the library is well known and respected for its traditional literacy initiatives, the library staff work tirelessly to encourage lifelong learning as essential to a vibrant community. As quantified below, the library practices community outreach beyond traditional library programming, services, and setting. With the aforementioned expansion, the library added ten members to its staff, and circulation, programming, and visitation grew. Otis Library currently has 44,000 members and logs 400 to 600 member visits each day. Despite the increase in daily use, however, government funding has decreased by 16 percent over the past four years. The rapid growth paired with reduced operating support has been a tremendous challenge, but it has

The nineteen flags decorating the interior of the Otis Library today represent the nationalities living in Norwich and using the facility.

also served as the catalyst for creative thinking that has led to a dynamic shift in how the library conducts its daily business.

Otis Library's modification in service began with a nine-stop community focus group tour that gathered business owners, students, families, new Americans, community leaders, and library supporters. Although it was the beginning of a larger dialogue about the service model, efficiencies, opportunities, and strengths, the conversation started with one fundamental change: the library held meetings off-site, taking the Otis Library outside its own four walls. That simple but profound shift changed the way Otis related to its community.

As a result, Otis Library now connects with many individuals and entities beyond its traditional space and service. The key to Otis's success stems from the thesis that Otis Library is an engaged partner that realizes a healthy, literate community is not just books, story times, and late fees housed on Main Street. The library and the community achieve success by listening and responding to needs and opportunities throughout town. Working to provide support for and enhancements to existing programs and events allows Otis Library and its partners to grow when financial limitations exist. The Otis works creatively to help fill the funding gap that many area partners have been simultaneously experiencing. For example, the library works collaboratively on grant opportunities with the school system, daycare providers, the senior center, and the parks and recreation department to provide opportunities that reach farther and create stronger outcomes. An active leader, advocate, communicator, and resource, Otis Library develops a pathway to aware, informed citizenship. Otis Library epitomizes the term *lifelong learner* with its clear commitment to provide enrichment at every stage of life.

The library also embeds the concepts of partnership and understanding within staff relationships. Although the library has content experts, Otis staff members are cross-trained in every area of service so that patrons can approach anyone and transactions are thorough and efficient. The library holds staff open forums monthly to bring concerns, celebrations, and information to the forefront. Otis's staff reflects a blending of longevity with professionals new to the field, resulting in a culture that utilizes its wide range of experience and perspectives to design and implement an innovative strategic plan.

In recognition of its service to the residents of Norwich and surrounding communities, the Otis Library won the National Medal for Museum and Library Service given by the U.S. Government's Institute of Museum and Library Services (IMLS) in 2016. The award ceremony occurred at the White House hosted by First Lady Michelle Obama and the institute's director, Dr. Kathryn K. Matthew. The library director, Robert Farwell, accepted the honor along with a member of the community. The IMLS received letters of support for the award nomination from Senator Richard Blumenthal of Connecticut and Eleanor O'Malley, the Norwich Office Coordinator for the nonprofit Literacy Volunteers of Eastern Connecticut, who cited the Otis's support for literacy programming and service to the area's growing foreign-born population. The library could have earned this high honor for its community services over one hundred years earlier, among the recent immigrants among the Falls Mills settlement population.

**The Future:** To a greater degree than other public libraries examined here, the future of the Otis Library is tied to the economic revitalization of Norwich at large and the downtown in particular—and vice versa. The library has the potential to serve along with the Norwich Free Academy (the private high school serving Norwich and surrounding communities) as the city's primary anchor institutions. Norwich's residents have lower rates of postsecondary education than surrounding areas of Connecticut as a whole and thus Otis's commitment to lifelong learning offers particular value to members of the community. Norwich was hit hard by the COVID-19 pandemic and daily attendance fell as community events were curtailed.

# McArthur Public Library

270 Main Street, Biddeford, ME

Established: 1863 (book collection) and 1902 (library building)

Benefactors: William P. Haines; Elizabeth Stevens, and Robert McArthur

The city of Biddeford, established in 1653, is a former mill town located on the Saco River, after which it was originally named, near where it flows into the Atlantic. The area is the site of one of the first European settlements in America. The population today is around 22,500 residents with a median household income of approximately $53,000. In its heyday Biddeford's cotton mills rivalled those in nearby Lawrence and Lowell in Massachusetts and brought many immigrants and prosperity to the area. Drawn by the growing number of mill jobs, many workers came beginning around 1850 from eastern Canada and by the turn of the century the proportion of native-French speakers was three out of five, higher than any other place in America. At this time Biddeford was Maine's fourth largest city. Today it has dropped to sixth, but it is growing again and has the youngest population of any city in the state, which overall has the most rapidly aging and oldest average population in the entire United States.

For many years the largest city employer in Biddeford was the Pepperell Manufacturing Company whose mills produced cotton fabric for tents and uniforms used by the Union Army during the Civil War and later became renowned for "Lady Pepperell" brand percale and muslin sheeting. Following WWI, the cotton mills and manufacturing shifted to factories in the South, negatively affecting Biddeford and other mill towns throughout New England.

However, in 1966, Pepperell introduced the Vellux blanket, developed and manufactured exclusively in Biddeford over some forty years in great secrecy. Oldtimers in Biddeford talk about how factory windows were blacked out during the mid-1960s both to protect the blankets from sunlight and some said to prevent prying eyes. These synthetic-fiber blankets became very popular and widely used both in homes and hotels worldwide given their durability and ease of cleaning. It is safe to say that many, if not most, Americans "of a certain age" have slept in beds with Lady Pepperell sheeting or Vellux blankets originally made in Biddeford. The blankets remain popular, but the patent and technology were sold to WestPoint Hospitality, based in South Carolina. Today, Biddeford's former factory buildings are filling with artists, publishers, IT firms, and high-tech startups.

**Library History:** The city was one of the first in Maine, and indeed New England, to enjoy a tax-supported public library when it first opened in 1863 as a city department led by the efforts of William P. Haines, then head of the Pepperell Mill. In 1881 a retired mill employee, Elizabeth Stevens, willed her life savings of $3,500 to provide a free public reading room. This led in 1895 to establishment by the city of the Biddeford Library and Reading Room Association and in 1902 it assumed responsibility for operating and maintaining the library. Concurrently, the association purchased a former church located on Main Street, establishing the McArthur Public Library. The library was named after Robert McArthur, the head of Pepperell since 1887, who led the process of negotiating and donating the funds for the purchase of the building. McArthur donated some $8,500 to assume the mortgage on the church.

He was an immigrant and a self-educated man who believed that public libraries provide all citizens with opportunities for advancement. He donated the major funding for the building as well as an endowment to support library operations and maintenance—a gift both his daughters repeated. McArthur also supported the construction of a modern public hospital in Biddeford and, upon his death, willed that the family home be turned into the city's home for the aged. McArthur's views on the value of public libraries and his generosity bring to mind another Scottish immigrant, Andrew Carnegie, who had similar views but had the means to support the establishment of public libraries across America during the same time frame (see Appendix IV).

Like in other towns and small cities in New England, a library association guides and supports the McArthur Public Library—a nonprofit, nongovernmental civil society organization led by a board of trustees. Public members of the board are elected each year at the association's annual meeting. Biddeford's mayor and school superintendent serve as ex officio members. A library committee from within the board membership is in charge of the library's general operation and management, setting policy while annually delegating responsibility for implementation to the library director. Library staff, including the library director, are employees of the association, not the city of Biddeford.

The McArthur Public Library main entrance. The former church steeple is at the right.

**The Physical Setting:** Although founded early in New England history, Biddeford does not have a town common, and instead its spatial typology is known as a crossroads town. United States Route 1 (Elm Street), which follows the Atlantic coastline the length of Maine. The McArthur Library sits on Main Street near its prominent intersection with Elm Street, just up the street from city hall in the heart of the reviving business district. The choice of the former church was also influenced by its proximity to the Pepperell and other mills, located just across the river, and their thousands of workers. The McArthur Library was a short distance away as the mill workers walked after work to their homes, often tenements built for the many young single women who made up the workforce. Recall that one such woman who benefited from access to the early library, Elizabeth Stevens, donated her life savings towards the establishment of a free public reading room.

This placement of many early public libraries in New England mill towns near factories and their workers is not uncommon nor insignificant. The location was designed to facilitate access and use by the working class and contradicts the impression that early libraries were only elitist institutions. This interest in helping to educate workers is also linked to the establishment of many libraries in the first place, motivated by a major employer in town, as seen in Biddeford as well as the featured cases of Lisbon, Athol, and Ashaway. In each case, not only did the employer donate construction funds, but they also gave the land that was inevitably nearby if not adjacent to the factory. One can only presume that the company owners wanted to provide their workers with the opportunity to self-educate and gain knowledge, which they could use later in life for advancement. This, of course, was the case not only of individual factory owners such as Haines and McArthur but also of Andrew Carnegie.

The library's exterior architecture is not remarkable; it looks like a former church even though a condition of the original deal was to remove the steeple to give the building a less religious look and feel. The building's interior is, as one could expect given its former life, somewhat disjointed and it can take newcomers a while to be able to navigate the corridors and rooms. The new main entry space and indeed the entire library is, however, a welcoming space for all.

Like many early libraries in town and city centers, the structure is not surrounded by car parking. For better or worse, this is an issue today with the lack of parking constraining the revival of the Biddeford downtown. City leadership understands this and recently completed a new parking structure a block off Main Street, a plan which the library supported and will benefit from.

**Library Use Today:** The McArthur Library is more than just a public library; it is the premier civic, cultural, and social institution in Biddeford, playing a key role in the small city's long-awaited renewal. It is important to reiterate that the library is a nonprofit, 501(c)(3) NGO and not a part of the municipal government. The FY 2019 Annual Report of the McArthur Library Association notes that nearly 92,000 patrons (ranging between 300 to 400 per day) used the library during the year, a 4 percent drop over the previous year, although the roughly 87,000 checkouts and renewals dipped 12 percent from the previous year. While the average age of Biddeford residents is considerably

The interior of the McArthur Public Library provides both use-based spaces and areas for individual reading.

younger than the Maine state average, the association estimated that usage by adults over thirty was around 60 percent of total patronage, and children under twelve comprise around 20 percent of users.

The majority of libraries featured in *Common Place* are experiencing the phenomena of greater patronage but with fewer books and other items in circulation. One explanation is that public libraries are attracting a larger proportion of patrons for programs, such as the wide array offered by the McArthur Library which has an extraordinary number for a library its size. Ongoing programs include, but are not limited to, children's, teen, and adult programming ranging from toddler time, drop-in kids' activities, Random Fandom for teens, Takes and Makes (craft and STEM kits), a thriving adult book group, and a number of public PCs and building-wide wireless. Library programs involve food insecurity and healthy eating; the site serves as a pick-up location for local farm share programs.

Recent special events have included genealogy help, adult crafts, a kids' and teen game and gadget drop-in, author and other talks (such as one by a professional astro-photographer), events cohosted with the Biddeford Historical Society, and Sunday afternoon concerts and outdoor movies (made possible through a recent grant of funding for audiovisual equipment from the Maine State Library's Public Library Fund and a local community partner). Patrons also use the library to conduct community meetings and to checkout nontraditional items ranging from sports equipment to snowshoes.

The McArthur Library Association particularly values community partnerships given its civil society status. These include six retirement homes and other facilities catering for an older adult population that benefit from delivery of library books, Biddeford's 50+ Club, and the local campus of the University of New England from which students volunteer to assist with community food insecurity programming.

Like libraries across America, the McArthur Library adapted its operations and programming in response to the pandemic. Many of these changes, such as increasing the library's reach virtually with digital offerings (and lending wifi hotspots), will be retained. Several of these efforts were featured in ALA publications and documents as good examples of what public libraries can do for their communities during periods such as this — and beyond.

The McArthur Library manages all of this with ten full-time and ten part-time staff. In addition, there is a thriving teen volunteer program. In spite of being an NGO, in FY 2022 44 percent of the approximately $1.2 million annual budget comes from the city — a figure that has been modestly growing in recent years. The balance of the budget comes mainly from endowments established by Robert McArthur's two children. Other grants are available from the Public Library Fund noted above and the Stephen and Tabitha King Foundation. Use of the library is free to all Biddeford residents, and patrons from surrounding towns pay a small membership fee.

The library director and board of trustees consider community support to be very strong, both among Biddeford residents at large and library users.

**The Future:** The library director's future plans include increased outreach, marketing, and awareness building conducted by a new staff member dedicated to this role, and provision of more public meeting spaces within the library. Greater "whole family engagement" will be supported. The children's room will be reoriented to greater "whole family" programming that encourage the entire family to attend together such as to enjoy "family read" programs. More broadly, library board officials noted two issues they plan to address in the coming years. In recent years the population of Biddeford has changed, with fifteen to twenty foreign languages (including French) spoken in homes, schools, and other social institutions. The most common native languages spoken by recent ESL students in the school system are Arabic, Portuguese, Kinyarwanda and Spanish. The library aims to encourage and facilitate use for recent arrivals with non-English native language.

Second, while the library's location smack in the middle of the business district served mill workers and those working or doing business downtown well in the past, today there is only a single public school within walking distance of the library. Biddeford no longer has a trolley system and the current form of public transportation does not offer comprehensive routes. The McArthur Library is thus addressing the fact that its original siting, intended to facilitate access to its original users, factory workers and other adults working downtown, is now a constraint in serving the youth of Biddeford. The library has increased outreach at schools; for example, for recent Summer Learning Programs. Communities across America have faced this same issue, with many larger communities responding by opening branch libraries in suburban locations that grew as a result of urban flight following WWII and, it must be said, civil right advances of the early 1960s.

## Ashaway Free Library

15 Knight Street, Ashaway, RI

Established: 1871

Benefactors: Hannah Cundall and Sylvia Salisbury;
and the Crandall family

Ashaway is a small village (population 1,195) located in the town of Hopkinton in the southwestern corner of Rhode Island near the border with Connecticut. The population has declined nearly 20 percent since 2010, but today households are younger and wealthier. The mean household income is $101,180 and the median household age is just under 38 years.

Ashaway was first settled around 1704. The village name is derived from the native American name for the river that runs through the area, the Ashawague, which means "land in-between." Like many towns and villages in New England the river served as the basis for the area's settlement and economic prosperity.

In the case of this village, the Ashaway Line & Twine Manufacturing Company sustained the local economy and much else, including the library. The company was founded in 1824 by Captain Lester Crandall who began the manufacturing of braided fishing lines made first of linen and then silk. The company continues today and is Rhode Island's oldest family-owned business and an example of Yankee ingenuity and American manufacturing innovation for nearly 200 years. In 1939 it was the first producer of a commercial nylon product—fishing line—when a then-young company, DuPont, was looking for a use for its new filament. In 1952, it became the first producer of Dacron fishing lines, and a few years earlier also began producing strings for tennis, squash, racquetball, and badminton rackets. Today it is a world leader and the only United States manufacturer of racket strings. Since 2004, it has been the manufacturer of the USA Racquetball Official String. It also manufactures high-tech medical threads for surgical use, Dacron backing and braided nylon cores for fly-fishing lines (made by companies such as Orvis), and last but not least, line for kites!

In 1970, when Ashaway Line's president, L. Robert Crandall, tragically passed away from amyotrophic lateral sclerosis (ALS), his widow, Pamela A. Crandall, previously a homemaker, enrolled in Connecticut College and graduated with honors in 1974. In 1976 she became Ashaway's President and later chaired the board and successfully led the company into the future. Upon her death in 2016, many cited her as a leader in the women's right movement of the 1970s and 1980s and noted that she was known and respected throughout Rhode Island as one of the most accessible small business executives, as well as a noted volunteer and philanthropist—including on behalf of the Ashaway Free Library.

The Crandall family is notable, aside from its support of the Ashaway Free Library. The patriarch, John Crandall (1618–1676) was a Baptist minister from England and one of the founding settlers of Westerly, Rhode Island. Prudence Crandall (1803–1890) was born in Hope Valley and became a schoolteacher and activist for women's suffrage and the rights of African Americans. Beginning in 1832, she admitted some twenty African American students to her school for girls in Canterbury, Connecticut, establishing what is thought to be the first integrated classroom in the United States. The school closed in 1834 after a public backlash. Robert Lloyd Crandall was born in neighboring Westerly in 1935 and became the CEO of American Airlines in 1985. Among his accomplishments while there, he created the first frequent flyer program in the airline industry. Other descendants of John Crandall include Julia Child, Lucille Ball, and Katharine Hepburn.

**Library History:** The Ashaway Free Library began in 1871 when two local ladies, Hannah Cundall and Sylvia Salisbury, donated books and contributed funding that resulted in a collection of about 650 volumes. The collection was housed in its own small building owned by the Ashaway Woolen Company, and the library association provided free and public access to the collection as well as an annual lecture series. In 1907 the library collection outgrew the structure, and local citizens purchased the former Ashaway kindergarten building (for $101) and to provide room for future expansion moved the schoolhouse (on log rollers) to the current site on the corner of Knight and High Streets. The Ashaway Woolen Company donated the property and Ashaway Line & Twine Manufacturing Company donated cash and later deeded additional land.

It was at this time that the library became known as the Ashaway Free Library, and shortly thereafter the original association reorganized as a nonprofit with a volunteer board of trustees including Horace L. Crandall as treasurer. This organizational structure remains today. The small library has had a number of librarians over the years, including Isaac Cundall, husband of one of the cofounders, and Lloyd R. Crandall. In 1951 the Ashaway Line & Twine Manufacturing Company President, L. Robert Crandall, became the president of the library board of trustees. He oversaw a major expansion of the library during the next fifteen years supported by community donations and matching funding from the Ashaway Charitable Trust, established in 1952 with major support from the Crandall family.

The original library building, then a kindergarten, before it was moved on log rollers to its current location.

**Physical Setting:** Ashaway does not have a town common or even a "Main Street," per se. The Free Library is, however, located on the prominent corner of Knight Street and High Street (Route 216) known locally as Library Hill, across the river and not far from the Ashaway Line & Twine Manufacturing Company headquarters and factory. The historic Jacob D. Babcock House (1778) is located across High Street, once the first Rhode Island station of the Underground Railroad. Babcock, the owner of the Ashaway Mill, and his wife, library cofounder Hannah Cundall, were committed abolitionists.

**Library Use Today:** The Ashaway Free Library continues to be operated as a nongovernmental organization, although approximately half of its annual budget comes from the town of Hopkinton. Interestingly, the town also provides similar support to another NGO-run public library, the Langworthy, in the larger village of Hope Valley some eight miles to the north. What sets the Ashaway Free Library apart from others highlighted in *Common Place* is that it is truly a very local, small village institution.

The Ashaway Free Library today.

The library currently has approximately 19,000 volumes and another 2,300 DVDs, CDs, and audiobooks and serves around 10,000 patrons per year. According to the town of Hopkinton history, written for the 1976 United States bicentennial, the library had approximately 10,000 volumes and an average monthly circulation of 1,200 books. Thus, we can see the collection has more than doubled in the last forty years, while use has declined some 25 percent as the record of prepandemic checkout per month was in the range of 860 books. During the pandemic average monthly circulation increased to 1,345, including e-materials. It is important to note, as in other libraries studied, that while book checkout is basically flat if not declining, patronage is not down as use of the library for community programs increases.

The library is part of the Ocean State Libraries system, giving users access to other books and resources statewide and throughout New England. The library is open thirty-six hours per week, has a part-time director and several librarians, and circulates around 17,000 items per year. There are three computer workstations and 24/7 wifi service in the building and grounds. There are approximately 5,000 logons per year.

The library's annual budget is about $120,000, of which a bit less than 70 percent currently comes from the town of Hopkinton and the state, with the town covering more than four times the contribution of the state. The state funding is tied to the town maintaining its own level of support. The remainder of the budget comes from local donations and some foundation support.

The board of trustees is comprised of village residents who volunteer for three-year terms, although there are no term limits and many community service-oriented members serve for several. There is no town representative on the board, as there is at Langworthy Library in Hope Valley. A recent board chairperson, Fran Cohen, noted there is no formal friends of the library group like in many other locations, but that an informal friends group does assist with the annual book sale and other fundraising efforts.

Led by its longtime director, Heather Field, the library conducted a community study and prepared a five-year plan in 2018. The study found the need for multiuse community space to better serve local populations including the elderly and disabled, households where English is a second language, and the underemployed. Half of the town's population do not have a college degree. Nearly 20 percent of the village population is over sixty-five years of age, and this proportion is growing. For both reasons there appears to be an interest in lifelong learning within the community.

**The Future:** The previous 2013 five-year plan resulted in the new mission statement of enriching the community by providing resources and related services and programming for personal skills, self-improvement, career advancement, cultural enjoyment, entertainment, and creative activities. It also resulted in a $300,000 capital improvement campaign to add a 700-square-foot multipurpose room to the library, increasing the size of the building by one-third as well as making the entire facility compliant with the Americans with Disabilities Act (ADA). The latter is especially important to older patrons who struggled with the walk from the parking in the rear to the front entrance. Library director, Heather Field, notes that the library has delivered books curbside to those that could not mount the front steps.

The new space, completed in 2019, provided room for individual and group work; book, craft, homework, and community groups, such as the Boy Scouts; lectures, art shows, performances, and films; and community services such as tax return preparation assistance. Construction was supported with small donations from area residents and funding from several foundations, including the Rhode Island–based Champlin Foundation and another originally founded with an endowment from owners of the Clicquot Club Company, regional makers of ginger ale during the first half of the 1900s, eventually purchased by Canada Dry.

A 2014 feature on the village in the *Providence Journal* noted that the Ashaway Free Library is a "cherished neighborhood institution." Through the efforts and foresight of the institution's small group of staff and community supporters, it is likely to remain so well into the future.

## Holyoke Public Library

250 Chestnut Street, Holyoke, MA

Established: 1870–1886

Benefactors: William Whiting, William Skinner, and J.P. Morgan

Holyoke is a small city first settled in 1655 and incorporated in 1873 located on the Connecticut River in western Massachusetts. It was first part of the large settlement of Springfield, known as Ireland Parish, and it today has an estimated population of just over 38,200 and a median household income of $40,769. It was one of the first planned industrial cities in America, and during its prime in the late-1800s it had the largest paper, silk, and alpaca wool mills in the world, producing some 80 percent of the writing paper in the United States. It was here that volleyball was invented in 1895 at the local YMCA chapter, and the city today is home to the Volleyball Hall of Fame.

Around 1850 the town constructed a dam and canal system, including electricity producing turbines, and the city's growth exploded. At its height, over twenty-five paper mills lined the canals, using logs floated down the Connecticut as a raw material. Between 1850 and 1890 the population of Holyoke increased by 1000 percent and by the outset of WWI had reached 62,000, with many who were skilled laborers working for the likes of the American Writing Paper Company, the Holyoke Machine Company (which made water turbines), and the foundry that cast the bronze doors to the United States Capitol Building.

Holyoke has always had an ethnically diverse, largely working-class population. In the 1890 census, it had the third most foreign-born residents per capita (47 percent) of any city in America. Following the Irish, others immigrated in the mid-1800s from Central and Eastern Europe as well as French-speaking parts of Canada.[24] In the second half of the twentieth century, people came largely from Puerto Rico and Latin America countries. In the 2010 census, Latinos formed 48.4 percent of Holyoke's population, reflecting the largest

Puerto Rican population per capita in the United States outside the territory itself.

Like many former industrial towns and cities in New England the socioeconomic characteristics of Holyoke dramatically changed during the past half-century and today the city is one of the most distressed in the region. The decade between 1970 and 1980 saw Holyoke lose nearly 11 percent of its population. Nearly 30 percent of the population lives below the poverty line, and that rate rises to around 45 percent for those under the age of eighteen. To this day Holyoke produces its own, less-expensive electricity from its power canal. Given this and the abundance of inexpensive former mill space, it is no surprise that in 2018 the first cannabis cultivation operation began, representing a ten-million-dollar investment and the prospect of a growth industry (pardon the pun) with low-skill employment opportunities.

**Library History**: In 1870 citizens of the city established the Holyoke Library Corporation with a collective donation of $3,000 and 1,200 books. William Whiting, age twenty-nine, became the first president. The library was public, although not free; subscribers paid a fee of one dollar per year (the same charge as the Otis Library in Norwich, Connecticut, established two decades earlier). The library's first home was in a room in an old school building on Appleton Street. In 1876 the library moved into a larger space in the newly built city hall at the corner of High and Dwight Streets in the heart of downtown. A decade later, the city amended its charter to allocate more funds to the library, and it became free to all residents. In the year that followed, the number of users jumped from 441 to 2,075. The deal between the city fathers and the major business interests reflected in the library corporation reflected the type of public-private partnership that became common in the Progressive Era. The nonprofit corporation continues to run the library to this day with some municipal support.

In 1897, near the height of the city's economic prosperity, the Holyoke Water Power Company offered the library corporation a full city block to erect a building, if in three years funds could be raised to do so. The corporation and citizens of Holyoke rose to the challenge and raised $95,000 with major donations from William Whiting, William Skinner, and J.P. Morgan.[25] The building architect, James A. Clough, offered his services for free. The impressive, large building opened to the public in 1902 and was dedicated as the People's College, which would have pleased Andrew Carnegie. A children's department opened, and overall circulation doubled within five years.

The newly built Holyoke Public Library centered in expansive grounds.

The library is unusual in that during 1912 a natural history museum opened within its walls, an arrangement which lasted until 1959. Like other urban libraries of the era, during the 1940s the library began to circulate phonograph records; by the end of the first week of this offering the shelves were bare! At its peak, record circulation rivaled that of books. By the end of the 1950s, when Holyoke's decline was starting, book circulation had reached 300,000 per year and three branches had been opened.

The 1970s and 1980s were very difficult decades for Holyoke due to the contraction of local industry. Municipal finances and philanthropic giving both suffered. In 1983 the friends of the library group began and soon grew to 400 citizen members. By the end of the 1980s an economic and financial crisis hit Holyoke, resulting in a 1989 municipal budget shortfall. The library shut its doors for a short time. The library tapped a portion of its then $1.5 million endowment to reopen and the friends of the library recruited thirty volunteers to assist the nontechnical aspects of library operations. Volunteerism has remained a lasting tradition at the Holyoke Public Library.

Due to deteriorating conditions at the library building, the historical collections moved out in 2005. This prompted a multimillion dollar grant proposal to renovate and expand the structure from the Massachusetts Board of Library Commissioners, contingent on the library corporation's success in gaining support from the city of Holyoke. Voters approved a $5.5 million municipal bond issue and, together with private donations, the project moved forward. The newly expanded and renovated Holyoke Public Library opened to the public in October 2013.

**Physical Setting:** Unlike many towns and cities in New England, modern (mid-nineteenth century on) Holyoke was a planned settlement based on a rectilinear street grid, with rectangular blocks making up downtown. (This in itself is remarkable given that motorized vehicles would not appear for another half-century.) There was no town common although there was some downtown open space including parks and athletic fields. The two largest of these, taking up an entire block each, are located between Maple and Chestnut Streets, roughly four blocks northwest of the closest of the power canals around which the mills and other factories sat.

The land for the 1902 library building, donated by the Holyoke Water Power Company (which developed modern Holyoke), was the westernmost of these two open spaces, the athletic park, on the dividing line between the urban zone's commercial and residential neighborhoods. The site, while spacious and generally well located, was some distance from the company worker housing neighborhood to the northeast between the power canals—a long walk, but still quite accessible if using a street trolley.

The building was on the northern end of the city block, and the other half became a park after two other planned buildings, to house art exhibits and a natural history museum, failed to materialize. The

The interior of the Holyoke Public Library blends the historic with the contemporary.

main entrance faced Maple Street, with brick townhouses on the other side. The architect designed a majestic neoclassical building constructed of Indiana limestone and white glazed brick. The rear of the building's interior contained the book racks, which patrons could browse after consulting the card catalogue. The shelving was black cast iron, and the floors were thick glass tiles permitting natural light to penetrate from the skylights to the lower levels.[26] In 1948 a donation allowed the library to commission of a series of murals depicting Holyoke's history, which took six years to complete.

**Library Use Today:** With the conclusion of the 2013 renovation and expansion, the library now also contains an inviting teen room, computer lab and classroom, quiet study and tutoring rooms, reading lounges, three meeting rooms, and a large community room for public meetings and events. Citizens use the quiet spaces for local business interviews or assistance with tax preparation. The community room has been used for job fairs. Wifi is available throughout the building. Some 115,000 patrons visit the library every year, averaging 300 to 350 per day, with more in the summer months.[27] About half of the users are adults and seniors over sixty-five years of age, who generally use the library in the morning. Another 30 percent are children and teens, who primarily come after school, with young adults making up the balance.

A full-time staff of eleven, assisted by eight part-time employees and a dozen volunteers[28] serve patrons, the number of which have grown since the 2013 work. Just over 18,950 Holyoke residents, or roughly half the population, have library cards, and in 2018 they checked out nearly 88,400 items, including 13,275 by nonresidents. Nearly 400 people per week use the library's thirty-four public access computers, including almost 2,800 hours per week of internet service. Library programs reached 5,270 patrons in 2018, a small decline from the 5,940 figure the previous year. The 2018 figure included 200 children who signed up for the Summer Reading Program.

An example of programming that reflects the city's current population and culture is the Friends of the Holyoke Library's *Saber es Poder* initiative that has served to strengthen the library's resources on Puerto Rican and Latin history, culture, and social movements. The inaugural event in 2018 was cosponsored by the Holyoke Community College and the Puerto Rican Cultural Project, a library board subcom-

Mini-golf in the library fund-raising event sponsored by the Friends of the Holyoke Public Library.

mittee. National Endowment for the Humanities and the Carlos Vega Fund for Social Justice, an initiative of the Community Foundation of Western Massachusetts, supported the event. The library's many programs cover a wide range of areas and topics, from local history and culture, to entertainment (films and musical events), author conversations, to children and teen offerings. Local businesses, the Spanish-language broadcaster Telemundo, and the local PBS affiliate, WGBY, based in nearby Springfield have all sponsored events.

The library board's thirteen members have never been locally elected. Rather, the library corporation appoints seven members, on the basis of a board nominating committee recommendations, and the city of Holyoke names six "City Director" members to the board. The original "old boys club" continued for one hundred years and failed to reflect the changing population of Holyoke. As late as 1985, all board members were white males, but today the board is much more diverse. Board members named by the mayor and approved by the city council must be residents of Holyoke. However, two of the three members who are Spanish speakers are not city residents, and thus were named by the corporation. The library director, who has held the position for over twenty years, was born in Puerto Rico, is female, and is a Holyoke resident. She reports her efforts and those of her staff to engage and fully serve Holyoke's large Puerto Rican population are strongly supported by both the corporation and city.

The library director cites strong community support for the Holyoke Public Library. Support from the city varies somewhat with the government and the economic conditions at the time. Except for the period in the late-1980s noted earlier, the city has maintained the level of financial support required by the policies of the Commonwealth of Massachusetts.

**The Future**: The library director anticipates the current growth trend will continue into the foreseeable future. Despite this view, her plan is to direct additional resources in the future for increased community outreach, including limited marketing costs. Another crucial use of additional revenue would be to increase library staff salaries. No staff has had a raise in salary in eleven years, which the board realized is affecting the library's competitiveness in hiring. However, in 2021 the Holyoke City Council updated the City Ordinance to include a revised Library Salary Schedule, increasing remuneration to a level comparable to other public libraries in the Commonwealth.

The long-time Friends of the Holyoke Public Library NGO was recently engaged in a reorganization effort, which is evaluating how the group can best serve the library while acknowledging demands on volunteers' time. This is an issue the library board is also grappling with, which is facing many friends of the library groups around America.

The library corporation plans to continue its fiscal prudence in managing the endowment, valued at the end of 2020 fiscal year at some $7.3 million, and is finalizing a new multiyear strategic planning effort covering both challenges and opportunities on the horizon.

## Guilford Free Library

4024 Guilford Center Road, Guilford, VT

Established: 1892

Benefactor: Cynthia King

Guilford is a small town in the southeastern corner of Vermont first settled in the mid-1700s. It is the only town in the United States chartered at one time or another in four different states, each of the first three one of the original thirteen colonies: Massachusetts (1732), New Hampshire (1754), New York (1758), and Vermont (1791). When Vermont joined the union, also in 1791, Guilford was the largest town in the state with a population of 2,430 and was known throughout the region as "the metropolis." It remained the most populous settlement in Vermont until 1820. 1791 marked the end of a nearly fifteen-year period of conflict between Yorkers and Vermonters concerning statehood. Basically, what is today Vermont was fought over by settlers and political leaders from the states of New Hampshire and New York. It was only in early 1777 that the territory declared its independence, before choosing the name Vermont. Between 1777 and 1791 Vermont was a sovereign state, but not one of the colonies, and for the first six months it was known as New Connecticut. Today Guilford has an estimated population of 2,120 and a mean household income of approximately $57,675.

The residents of Guilford have always lived on small farms practicing agriculture. Because there is no river of any large size within the town, nor a railway line, there has never been industry except for small lumber mills and blacksmithing shops. Guilford may be one of only a few towns in America whose population was at a high point when it began. Nearby Brattleboro, located on the Connecticut River, immediately attracted residents away, and in 1890 the population had dropped to 870. The nadir was in 1930 when the census counted only 663 residents. Between 1960s and 1980s there was an influx of residents with population increases of between 25 percent to nearly 40 percent per decade. Many newcomers during this period were members of the "counterculture," as local town historians later characterized them. In fact, by the mid-1970s one out of seven town residents lived on one of the several local communes. This is likely one of the highest proportions ever found in the United States.

Guilford has never been particularly known for anything other than some of its people. Wilber Fisk (1792–1839) was a prominent Methodist minister and the first in New England to have a college degree from Brown University in 1815. He went on to become the first President of Wesleyan University in Middletown, Connecticut, in 1831. Another Guilford native, Hosea Ballou II (1796–1861), followed these footsteps. He became a prominent Universalist minister and became the first (1853–1861) President of Tufts University, established in Medford, Massachusetts, and the first Universalist named to the Harvard College Board of Overseers. He was named after his uncle, who was called by some the father of the Universalist Church. The Universalists were the social progressives of the day, being committed abolitionists, believing strongly in the separation of church and state, and among the first denominations to ordain a woman in 1863. Other prominent Universalists from New England included Clara Barton, founder of the American Red Cross; P.T. Barnum, of circus fame; and Ted Sorensen, JFK's special counsel and speechwriter. In 1961, the Universalist Church joined the American Unitarian Association to form the Unitarian Universalist Association.

Not all famous Guilford native sons and daughters were ministers. John Wolcott Phelps was born in 1813 and graduated from West Point in 1836. He served in the Army and retired, but reenlisted in 1861, commissioned as a General, and led the recruitment of volunteer troops for the Union Army—Vermont being the first state to do so. Within a month of his receiving his new commission, Phelps called for freed blacks to serve as soldiers in the Union Army. Superiors disagreed, and he was forced to resign in August 1862. However, within two years President Lincoln issued the Emancipation Proclamation and asked Phelps to be the chief officer in command of the black troops. Phelps declined, insisting as a matter of principle that he be granted back pay, which Lincoln declined to authorize. Phelps was the only Vermonter to become a presidential candidate, in 1880, until Howard Dean (2004) and Bernie Sanders (2016 and 2020) followed suit.

While not a native daughter, Lucy Terry Prince lived in Guilford with her husband, Abijah Prince, from 1764 to 1803, raising all their six children.[29] Her story is truly remarkable. Terry was born in West Africa, kidnapped, and survived the Middle Passage as an infant, and was sold into slavery in Rhode Island and later the frontier town of Deerfield, Massachusetts. Prince, a freed former slave from Curacao, purchased Terry's freedom and married her in 1756. Terry's accomplishments are extraordinary. She produced the oldest known work of literature by an African American of either gender; a ballad about an attack by native Americans against the white settlers in Deerfield. She was the first woman of any race to have addressed the Supreme Court of the United States in the late-1790s. One son, Cesar, fought in the Revolutionary War. Another, Festus, sought admittance to Williams College. Although unsuccessful, Terry delivered a lengthy address to the college board of trustees that was noted for its eloquence and skill, echoing Supreme Court Associate Justice Samuel Chase's remarks following her winning case that her argument was better than he had heard previously from any lawyer from Vermont. This is all the more notable given that Terry never had the opportunity for formal education. While there is no historical record, it is entirely plausible that Terry was one of the card-carrying patrons of Guilford's original public library. Terry passed away at age ninety-seven in 1821 in Sunderland, Vermont, today home of Orvis, a wilderness outfitter beloved by fly-fishermen and dog owners. An obituary in the Greenfield, Massachusetts, newspaper, *The Franklin Herald*, noted, "In this remarkable woman there was an assemblage of qualities rarely to be found among her sex."

In more modern times Guilford's most famous resident is surely the classical pianist, Rudolf Serkin, who fled Hitler with his family in 1939 and settled on a local dairy farm in the mid-1940s. Serkin is known for his Beethoven interpretations, receiving among other awards the Presidential Medal of Freedom at the White House from JFK in 1963. In 1951 Serkin, with his father-in-law, Aldolf Busch (who lived on an adjacent farm in Guilford), founded the Marlboro Music School and Festival in the town just north of Guilford. The school and festival, located on the campus of Marlboro College, have had a significant influence on chamber music in America. The Guarneri Quartet was formed at Marlboro in 1964, and a decade later Yo-Yo Ma met his wife, Jill, while both were in summer residence at the festival. In August 1961, the two hundredth anniversary of the first settler's arrival in Guilford, Serkin organized a classical concert on his farm for all the town residents. He passed away on his farm in 1991, aged 88.

**Library History:** During the heydays of the 1790s, the Guilford Social Library began in the hamlet of East Guilford with 300 volumes—the first public library in Vermont. It remained open until 1818, when the town's population had declined by one-quarter. The next public library was proposed one hundred years later, in 1890, with a donation of $1,000 for the purchase of books left in the will of Cynthia King (known as Aunty King), if the town provided a building. The historical records in Guilford do not say more about King, other than that her will also provided for improvements to the town cemetery and meeting house. She was the wife of Chauncey King, who descended from William King who arrived in Salem, Massachusetts, in 1635 from England.

Another resident, William W. Barney, donated the necessary land the next year and the town contributed $300 for the cost of construction by George W. Franklin. The Guilford Free Library opened its doors on July 2, 1892 with 575 volumes. Records indicate that in the first year nearly 150 library cards were issued and that 1,300 books were checked out. The following year, the collection jumped to 800 volumes. The Free Library's board of trustees had five members, including selectmen. From the beginning the library took and returned books for shut-ins in conjunction with the Guilford Community Church established in 1770. It also established a close relationship with the Guilford Central School librarian.

**Physical Setting:** Given its hilly topography, Guilford never had a town common or a downtown. The very rural town consists of several small hamlets, including a small commercial hub around the intersection of the main north-south highway through the town (Route 5) and Guilford Center Road. Arguably, the heart of the town is located several miles up this road to the west, and it is here in Guilford Center that the Free Library, the historic community meeting house, and the Broad Brook Grange Hall, erected in 1884, are clustered together. It is notable that the corner lot donated for the library is immediately adjacent to the meeting house, built in 1822 as the first town hall, now on the National Registry of Historic Places.

The Guilford Free Library today. It is the smallest of the public libraries highlighted in *Common Place*.

The Guilford Free Library building is tiny and appears almost as a dollhouse, especially when viewed adjacent to the much larger meeting house. Taken together these two building serve the community well. Why expand the library to add public meeting space, as many public libraries such as the Ashaway Free Library have done, when that space is already a few steps away? The book collection contains works for both adults and children, but the book collection, programming and the intimate scale of the interior all seem geared for early readers.

**Library Use Today:** The Free Library is part of the Guilford town government, but also serves residents of the adjacent largely rural town of Halifax which has no library of its own. In a typical week 25–40 patrons utilize the library. More young families are residing within Guilford and children under twelve years comprise along with seniors the single largest proportion of patrons, at roughly 35 percent each. Teenagers use the Free Library the least, as they have access to school libraries.

The town provides approximately 80 percent of the annual budget, recently about $48,000 for staff, with the balance used for programming raised by the Friends of the Library NGO. All library staff are town employees. The library director works 20 hours per week and her assistant about half of that. There are also three volunteers who work as needed. Trustees are elected for five-year terms; the current chair has served as a trustee for 33 years.

In addition to providing normal library services the Free Library publishes using volunteer help the *Guilford Gazette*, a quarterly community newspaper. The library hosts periodic "folding parties" to get the publication out. The library also itself publishes a monthly newsletter highlighting upcoming programs and recent additions to the collection. Each year there is a Halloween celebration with books distributed as "treats." The Free Library volunteers help to deliver books to shut-in residents living at home and twice a month serve patrons at the senior living facility located in town.

Regular Free Library programs include summer reading camps for young people with various sessions covering grades K-8. Middle and high schoolers (and usually alumni) are recruited as "helpers." On a weekly basis, supported by the Friends the library offers "storytime" for pre-schoolers, "back roads stories" and a book club meeting once a month for older patrons. Home-schooling is relatively widely practiced in Guilford and for half the day on Fridays the library is dedicated to the use of these families. In addition to books (and audiobooks) the Free Library loans home medical devices and winter sports equipment.

**The Future:** The Free Library works closely with other voluntary community organizations such as the Guilford Cares Group, Community Collaboration for Guilford and the community center now operating just down the street at the former Grange Hall, which offers meeting space. The library often opens "after hours" for use by members of these groups and others. The library director noted that the facility largely meets the needs of the town, but that a second story addition is the one major item in the trustee's longer-term plans for the Free Library. The additional space would be used for town historical collections and "quiet space" as the current facility lacks any area where study can occur without the potential for distraction.

## Bridgton Public Library

1 Church Street, Bridgton, ME

Established: 1895

Benefactor: Dr. Nathan J. Davis and Clara Fogg

Bridgton is a small town, first settled in 1768 and incorporated in 1794, located in south-central Maine in the state's scenic Lakes Region. Names of adjoining towns, Sweden and Denmark, offer a sense of the early settlers. The main highway (Route 302) passes through the town to the White Mountains just across the border with New Hampshire. The town today has an estimated population of 5,200 and a mean household income of approximately $47,000, the lowest level among the library case studies. Bridgton has, however, a low cost of living and is attractive to retirees. The local economy benefits from summer vacationers, including vacation homeowners, and tourists passing through year-round.

The early town had about a dozen mills producing cut lumber, woolen textiles, shoes, bricks, shovel handles, and coffins. In 1832 a canal opened, connecting the town with the city of Portland, and the local economy and the population grew accordingly. In 1883 a small-gauge railroad link was completed, and summer vacationers began arriving. The importance of education to early residents is evidenced in the Bridgton Academy, which was established in North Bridgton in 1808 when the entire town had a population of only around 800 and today is an all-male college preparatory school.

The popular author Stephen King, born in Bangor, spent his teenage years in the area, and today has a home nearby. Bridgton is the setting for *The Mist*, a novella written by King, and is the inspiration for Chester's Mill, the main town in his book *Under the Dome*.

**Library History:** The progenitor of town's public library was the Bridgton Library Society, established in about 1820 by the Reverent Nathan Church, the first pastor of the only church in Bridgton. This reading society had seventy-five initial members, eleven of whom were women. The dues were twenty-five cents per year. The rules governing the society noted, "Conversations with books, accompanied with suitable meditations, greatly refines as well as pleases the mind and renders men nearer to the rank and privileges of superior beings." A decade later the society merged with the Youth's Library Society to form the Union Library Society. This civil society group appears to have lasted until approximately 1845. Another reading society sprang up in 1854, and in 1876 the group established the Central Reading Room in a building on the town square. The group's bylaws prohibited several vices: smoking, gambling, and political discussion of any sort.

In August 1895 the Bridgton Public Library was founded, receiving a charter from the state of Maine as a "Social and Literary Library to be established at Bridgton Center Village." While open to the public, the library did not become free until 1941 when the group modified its bylaws. The first chairman of the civil association responsible for the library was also the librarian, Dr. Frank Stevens. He was a druggist and the book collection was in his pharmacy until it moved to a vacant room in another building in 1898. Just two years later, a women's association raised and donated funds for a new library building on a lot donated by a Clara Fogg.

A local physician, Nathan Johnson Davis, wished to give something to the youth of his native town, and in his will provided $10,000 for erection of a public library building in memory of his son, Dalton Homes Davis, who predeceased him at the age of twenty-four years. The executors of the will established a trust with an $8,000 endowment to help operate the library and in 1913 the Dalton Holmes Davis Memorial Library opened its doors to the public with Dr. Davis's large book collection as its centerpiece. Later that same year, a former Maine Governor contributed his collection of nearly 900 volumes.

From its founding in 1895, the library has been a nonprofit, civil society organization. In spite of the endowment income, the library closed its doors for lack of funding during the height of the Great Depression, but it was able to reopen less than six months later when the town of Bridgton began supporting the library at the rate of $500 per year. Records indicate this support grew to $25,000 per year by 1994.

Major milestones of the library during its more recent history include a revision of the bylaws in 1971 to allow students to serve on the board of trustees, the first running in 1977 of the "4 on the Fourth" annual fundraising race to support the children's reading room, the establishment in 1980 of the Friends of the Bridgton Public Library, drafting of modern articles of incorporation (as a "literary and social library") in 1990 to obtain nonprofit status for tax purposes, and associated changes to the bylaws made in 2002.

**Physical Setting:** The library building is situated on the corner of Church and Main Streets (Route 302) in the village center. Across Church Street is a museum that sits along a stream that connects two of the many lakes in the town. In terms of appearance and size the building could be mistaken for one of the many Carnegie libraries erected during the same period across the country. Designed by an architect from Lewiston, Maine, it is a single-story structure of brick with stone trim. Like many library designs of that day, the origi-

The Bridgton Public Library, located on Main Street (Route 302).

nal wood-paneled interior has the librarian's circulation desk in front of the main entry off of Main Street, with reading rooms to either side and the book stacks to the rear. The building was added to the National Registry of Historic Buildings in 1989.

A major renovation and expansion was completed in 1993 at a cost of $350,000. The basement now holds a sizable community meeting room and the large children's books section, with the addition of an elevator ADA compliance. Grant funding for this project came from the Maine State Library, the Maine Historic Preservation Commission, the town of Bridgton, and donations from the friends of the library, numerous individuals, a local foundation, and an FHA loan. The library purchased adjacent properties on Church Street in 1991 and 1999 for library parking.

**Library Use Today:** The library has an average of roughly 480 patrons per week. It varies by month, as during the summer visitors at nearby vacation homes increase use—in July an estimated 34 percent of patrons are not year-round residents. This number works out to about 4.8 visits per full-time resident per year, a bit lower than the Maine average for all public libraries of 5.89 in 2017.

Book circulation peaked in 2010 when 43,236 books were checked out. The figure had dropped to 26,000 by 2016. Overall library usage has not declined as much since participation in programs has increased. Popular offerings include a tot book hour, tech help service, and a large book club. The patrons use public computers and the free Wi-Fi service, which is accessibly from the rear parking area as well.

The library has a staff of three, including its director, each of whom work thirty-two hours per week. Members of the Friends of the Bridgton Public Library also volunteer when needed. The operating budget is around $200,000 per year, of which approximately 40 percent comes from the town. It is interesting to note that when the town began supporting the library in 1937, the amount was $500 out of an overall budget of $750. Over the decades that followed, the proportion of library support in the town budget has significantly declined.

The remainder of funding comes from the library's endowment (no more than five percent of the current market value of the invested funds) managed by the board of trustees, local fundraising, the major "4 on the Fourth Race" (which annually raises about $30,000), and in-kind gifts and grants from the friends of the library.

The friends, with a dozen dedicated core members, run a book shed selling used books and conduct an annual sale, which generates around $750 in donations to the library. For 2018, the overall estimated value of support from the friends was nearly $10,000.

The library's bylaw permits up to fifteen members on the board of trustees, although there are normally a dozen members. Terms are for three years, and members are nominated by town residents, vetted by the board, and then voted on by the current members.

Library leadership characterizes community support as strong (users) to moderate (larger community). The friends and board both play an important role in advocating for library use and support.

**The Future:** Somewhat unusually, especially for Maine, the town population is increasing but at the same time, growing older. Most of the increase in population is attributed to retirees moving to the area. This demographic is reinforced by the fact that Bridgton currently has the lowest mean household annual income of any of the case study locations, at just under $47,000. These are fixed incomes. What is notable is that while the population is not wealthy by any means, the trustees have done a commendable job of soliciting numerous, if relatively small, individual bequests from wills. This trend will likely continue as average age of the population grows.

Serving this population means both maintaining book inventory, including adding more large-print and audiobooks as eyesight among some users grows weaker, and addressing an increased demand for nonbook services and programs that will help residents, especially the elderly, to get connected. If funding were available, likely from foundation grants, the leadership would prioritize advocacy and outreach about the library's programs and services and providing transportation to elderly users with limited mobility.

## Kellogg-Hubbard Library

135 Main Street, Montpelier, VT

Established: 1896

Benefactors: Martin M. Kellogg and John E. Hubbard

Montpelier is the state capital of Vermont and was first settled in 1787 and officially chartered as a village in 1818 and as a city in 1895. The city is located in the north-central part of the state and has an approximate population of 7,850 and a mean household income of around $68,125. It is the least populous state capital in America, although the workweek population nearly triples due to the number of government jobs held by workers from surrounding communities.

The original settlers came from Massachusetts shortly after the conclusion of the Revolutionary War, and the town's name was chosen in honor of the support of France in gaining American independence. Vermont joined the union in 1791, and in 1805 the state legislature chose Montpelier as the capital, given its central location and gifts of land and money from some local promoters. By the mid-1800s a railroad reached the growing town and manufacturing grew alongside government, driven by ample hydropower from the confluence of three rivers near the center of Montpelier. The modern town street layout was in place by 1860, and in 1884 it became the first town in the state to install a municipal hydroelectric system to power streetlights.

Montpelier's history is notable for devastating floods that occurred in 1927 and again in 1992, both of which affected the Kellogg-Hubbard Library. The first flooding incident affected all of Vermont and is considered the worst in state history, comparable only to the great hurricane of 1938 and Hurricane Irene in 2011. The three-day downpour in November 1927 killed some eighty-five people, including the lieutenant governor of the state. Loss to property was also huge, equivalent to roughly $5,800 per resident in 2018 dollars, but long before people carried flood insurance. It is said that during the 1938 hurricane, salt spray was seen on windows in Montpelier in spite of the fact it is 120 miles from the coastline! The 1992 flooding, in contrast, occurred when an early spring thaw formed an ice dam on the main river flowing through Montpelier, flooding the entire downtown area and causing millions in damage. The flood did not spare the public library.

Montpelier has a few famous native sons and daughters and one is George Dewey (1837–1917), the hero of the Battle of Manila Bay during the Spanish-American War. He was the only man in United States history named Admiral of the Navy. He was a descendent of Thomas Dewey who was born in Kent, England, in 1603 and died in 1648 in Hartford, Connecticut. This line of the Dewey family tree is no relation to either the educator/philosopher John Dewey, nor Melvil Dewey, the creator of the Dewey Decimal System and co-founder of the American Library Association. Other natives include Tony Award-winning playwright Anais Mitchell and Senator Patrick Leahy who has a special relationship to the Kellogg-Hubbard as noted below.

**Library History:** The first library in Montpelier was a small social library of 200 volumes that began in 1794. The Village Library Society operated between 1814 and 1850, and in 1860 the Agricultural Library opened. This corresponded with a surge in the city's population to over 3,200 residents. It provided two reading rooms, newspapers, magazines, and circulating books free to the public. It closed its doors in 1880. As the name of today's Montpelier public library may hint, its founding in the early 1890s was a saga that rocked the city and ultimately involved individuals from afar including a United States Supreme Court Justice, John Marshall Harlan. The saga began in 1889 when Mr. and Mrs. Martin Kellogg passed away within three months of each other. They had jointly decided in their wills to leave their sizable estate of $300,000 to the city for several purposes, including the erection of a public library. When Fanny Kellogg died shortly after her husband, her only living relative, nephew John E. Hubbard, contested the will. He was the only son in a family that was at one time the largest real estate owner in Montpelier, and whose father had helped finance the largest hotel in the city and the Vermont State House after the first building had burnt down in 1857. A judge in New York City, where the Kellogg couple had lived, agreed with Hubbard, but the city countersued. The dispute lasted for three years, and the case was heading to the supreme court of Vermont when John Hubbard agreed to build a library for $30,000, if the city dropped its case.

The city agreed, but the deal enraged many of the city's current and even former residents. John W. Burgess, a Montpelier native and friend of Martin Kellogg, became a key player. He had become a constitutional law professor at Columbia University in New York City. Some, including Burgess, charged that money had changed hands to sweeten the deal. Nevertheless, an elegant two-story granite library building, ultimately costing $60,000 of Hubbard's money, was designed, built, and opened in early 1896 with 5,600 volumes. However, Burgess was still aggrieved and turned to a rival subscription library run since 1885 by the local YMCA and the Montpelier Public Library Association (MPLA).[30] Burgess stated that this group would "stand up as a permanent protest against the settlement by the lawyers and officials of the town in the Kellogg will case and against condoning of the offense by the community."

Another native son then joined the local battle. Thomas Waterman Wood was a renowned artist who then was president of the National Academy of Design in New York City. Wood was close to Burgess, as Burgess's wife was both a student of and assistant to the artist, who was then in his 70s. Wood offered to deed to the city over forty of his paintings, valued at some $30,000, provided the city's books be kept at the MPLA library rather than the Kellogg-Hubbard building. In other words, another bribe. In August 1895 the MPLA library displayed donated paintings at an opening attended by United States Supreme Court Justice Harlan,[31] one of the United States senators from Vermont, the president of the University of Vermont, and a Roman Catholic Bishop. In spite of this showy anti-Hubbard event, Hubbard's library opened to the public in January of 1896. The same year, the MPLA library was made free to the public. Wood sought and received a court order preventing the city from giving the MPLA library book collection to the Kellogg-Hubbard library. However, in 1899 the books were merged with the Kellogg-Hubbard collection.

Controversy raged during the next three years around the dueling libraries and only ended in mid-1899 when John Hubbard suddenly died at age fifty-one, supposedly of liver cancer. Many thought the battle stress of the past decade played a role. Some hinted at supernatural justice, pointing to a violent storm that passed over the city in the hours before Hubbard's death: "word ran through town that, in the midst of the tornado, the spirit of Hubbard had departed." The lengthy obituary in the local paper was more sympathetic, and in a separate article the same day hinted that Hubbard's final will and testament would be surprising to all, including his numerous detractors. Sure enough, it soon revealed that the vast bulk of his $300,000 estate was left to Montpelier, including $125,000 to expand hours of operation and endow the Kellogg-Hubbard library for the future.[32] Hubbard also gave Montpelier some one hundred acres of prime land overlooking downtown for a public park. As noted in a historic account written in 2000, his bequest paralleled the Kellogg will he had contested a decade before.

The newly constructed Kellogg-Hubbard Library building in 1904.

As things turned out, in 1948, the trustees of the Wood Art Gallery approached the Kellogg-Hubbard board about moving the art collection into the library. In 1953 the gallery opened on the second floor and the collection remained until 1985 when it was relocated to Vermont College. A replica of the famous Elgin Marble frieze from the Parthenon remains to this day across the upper walls of the second story main room, now full of book stacks, along with two other historic friezes.

A short time after this controversial beginning, the Kellogg-Hubbard faced financial difficulties. The Montpelier selectmen denied support in 1898, but the next year when faced with the library's closure they voted to give $2,000 provided the Kellogg-Hubbard be wholly transferred to the city. The library trustees refused, and the institution closed its doors. The local Ladies' Library Guild, reorganized as the Ladies' Library League, donated resources and the Kellogg-Hubbard reopened after fourteen weeks. What is significant is that the board of trustees felt so strongly about maintaining the Kellogg-Hubbard's independence and as several *Common Place* case studies note, that once again it was the women of the local community who demonstrated support for the public library.

The 1927 flood, mentioned earlier, almost destroyed the entire book collection. Sixty-five years later, the 1992 ice dam flooding swamped the basement children's room, but staff and community volunteers were able to save nearly 20,000 books from permanent destruction. To avoid similar problems in the future, in 1998 library trustees decided to relocate the children's room to a new addition and to renovate the entire building. In 2001 the new wing, named after United States Senator Patrick J. Leahy, opened housing the children's book collection.

Senator Leahy was born and raised in Montpelier and visited the Kellogg-Hubbard during the 1940s and 1950s on a nearly daily after-school basis. He spent many hours in the basement children's library which opened in 1951 when the Senator was 11 years old reading through the collection of books by authors such as Dickens and

Robert Louis Stevenson. Besides his love of reading, Senator Leahy is fond of two other things of note: The Grateful Dead and comics — especially Batman. He was on friendly terms with the late Jerry Garcia and other former band members. Senator Leahy has also written for, acted in, and done voiceovers for several Batman television episodes and movies, including *The Dark Knight*. In each case, the senator has had the residuals and royalties sent to the Kellogg-Hubbard for purchase of additional books for the children's library.

Congressional Record

Senate

KELLOGG-HUBBARD LIBRARY

Senator Patrick Leahy regarding his fond childhood memories of the library and in particular the children's librarian.

**Physical Setting:** The library is situated in a prominent downtown location on the corner of Main and School Streets, across from the Unitarian Universalist Church, and a short walk away from the state house. It is on the very edge of the downtown commercial district, and within a few short blocks are located two schools. Its central location and accessibility ensure lunch hour, after-school, and evening use.

The original two-story building is designed in the Classical Revival style, popular at the time, and constructed from rough granite quarried nearby. It's proportions are palatial, and it was clearly intended to be a monument not to a single individual or family "but the progress, prosperity and democratic ideals of the capital city."[33] The principal entrance on Main Street is flanked by four columns. The structure features rounded bays and ample windows with unusual portholes under the roof eaves. A central skylight also provides additional natural lighting.

The major 2001 work added nearly 6,400 square feet to the structure in a manner sensitive to the original building, which is on the

National Register of Historic Places and is located near the heart of Montpelier's designated Historic District. The financing of over $2.6 million was supported by a wide range of sources. The town meeting overwhelmingly voted for a $600,000 bond issue, and four of the five towns also serviced by Kellogg-Hubbard also approved major contributions totaling $200,000. Individual contributions totaled $425,000 and local businesses and organization contributed over $225,000. Grants from the state and foundations donated $100,000, and another $330,000 came from the library endowment. Finally, the library obtained two federal grants totaling $750,000 with the support of Senator Patrick J. Leahy.

**Library Use Today**: The Kellogg-Hubbard serves Montpelier and the five other surrounding towns—Berlin, Calais, East Montpelier, Middlesex, and Worcester—with a total population of approximately 17,000. It is the only multi-jurisdiction library in the case studies in this book.[34] During 2018, an average of 3,900 patrons visited the library every week, or roughly 700 per day. Circulation of physical items and digital downloads are on the order of 300,000 per year. This high level of usage has been constant over the past two decades.

According to the library director, the highest proportion of patrons are over-65 seniors, at roughly 30 percent, followed by children under twelve years at about 25 percent, many of whom are involved with programs. Preschool-aged children come in the mornings with parents for play or story time. Adults between the ages of twenty to thirty and thirty to sixty-five years both represent 20 percent. Teenage users, who checkout books, use the internet, and just hang out, comprise the remaining 10 percent. Many older adults and senior use the Kellogg-Hubbard for evening programs and meetings. Many elementary and middle school kids come unattended after school lets out and walk home or are picked up by parents in the late afternoon.

The library's onsite collection is over 72,000 items, including books, DVD, and CDs, while the Vermont interlibrary loan service provides access to many others, and the Vermont Online Library provides access to materials through nearly sixty databases. There are fourteen computers for public use and free Wi-Fi throughout the building. Librarians offer assistance on using the internet for research, pleasure, and downloading thousands of ebooks and audiobooks onto personal devices.

The Kellogg-Hubbard has a long history of offering community programs and meeting space. Today, of over 500 programs per year, the majority are for children and young adults, with an estimated patronage of nearly 10,000 area residents. In 1980 the library began a thematic reading discussion series sponsored by the Vermont Humanities Council. Local scholars present books and facilitate discussions on a wide variety of topics. This Athenaeum-like program continues today. Now known as First Wednesdays, the program, funded in part by the Institute of Museum and Library Services and three statewide underwriters, functions in nine libraries around Vermont, including the Kellogg-Hubbard where is it also supported by a number of local sponsors. Recent events have covered topics such as "fake news," and democracy in America, the legacy of Rachel Carson, and the architecture of Montpelier.

Community life in Montpelier is vibrant and the Kellogg-Hubbard Library serves with this notice post board and as an event venue.

PoemCity, the library's month-long celebration of poetry, marked its tenth anniversary in 2019. The program is supported by the Council on Humanities, Vermont College of Fine Arts, the Poetry Society of Vermont, as well as private sector businesses. While the library is the program originator and producer, poems are read or displayed in many Montpelier and surrounding town locations (including bus stops) and even Vermont's Welcome Centers located on the major highways leading into and out of the state! The 2019 kickoff event featured Madeline Kunin, former three-term governor of Vermont, who read poems from her memoir as well as forthcoming work.

The library employs five full-time and seven part-time staff, led by two Co-Directors. The board of trustees has fifteen seats, two of which are for members nominated by the Montpelier City Council, and another five for members representing the surrounding towns served by the Kellogg-Hubbard. The board reflects the diversity of the communities and patrons served, although finding younger members able to commit the amount of time required for this working board has been a challenge at times. As a result, until recently few members had young children in the household. However, a recent board president remarked (at age seventy-four) that grandparents do a pretty good job of looking out for the needs and interests of young library users!

The Friends of the Kellogg-Hubbard Library was first established in 1958, but quickly waned before being reinvigorated in 1961 to help raise funds and increase the book collection. The friends group revitalized again in 1993 following the board of trustees' decision to name a community representative to the board and open its meetings to members of the public. This action followed growing public concerns about the governance of the Kellogg-Hubbard, and a local ballot initiative in 1992, which called for appointment of a public representative to the board. The nonbinding measure passed 2,545 to 850. The lack of public representation had caused the Kellogg-Hubbard to be the only large library in the state to fail Vermont Department of Library certification. Today there is no active friends group, but community residents volunteer to support fundraising and other ad hoc tasks under the direction of library staff. Examples include book deliveries to local daycare and preschool facilities (where volunteers also read) and to senior living centers and homebound patrons.

The Kellogg-Hubbard's operating budget for FY 2022 is $918,000, of which member municipalities contribute 54 percent. In Montpelier residents vote on the library's annual budget allocation, with typically 80 to 85 percent voting in favor of the proposed allotment. Four of the five surrounding towns have similar levels of financial support, with the remaining one conflicted by some residents' use of other libraries in the adjacent towns of Barre and Northfield. Another 25 percent of the annual budget comes from endowment interest, and nearly 20 percent from donations and fundraising events. Nonresident fees, fines, and miscellaneous income make up the balance. Kellogg-Hubbard leadership characterizes community support as strong, with among the highest patronage and fundraising in Vermont.

**The Future:** Library staff anticipates that patronage of the Kellogg-Hubbard will increase over the coming five-year period, including physical item circulation which has, contrary to most other case study libraries in *Common Place*, grown over the past five years. In terms of digital content, the forecast is that as more online material from other sources becomes located behind paywalls, demand for digital library offerings, including digital periodicals, audiobooks and streaming video, will also increase. The Kellogg-Hubbard's extensive programming will maintain if not increase, but to do so will require additional resources. Other use of such resources include increased hours of operations. Saturday hours, currently 10 am to 2 pm, may extend or Sunday hours added. The library may also add additional after-school programming for kids.

The longtime Kellogg-Hubbard Library executive director retired in 2019 and was replaced by two Co-Directors, a rarity among public libraries. These appointments, approved by the board of trustees, reflected a renewed commitment to innovate. The new Co-Directors have a combined nineteen years of time at the Kellogg-Hubbard, serving respectively as the director of library services and director of finance and operations. Both have graduate degrees, one in library and information sciences and the other in higher education administration. This breadth of experience is especially valuable in a library such as the Kellogg-Hubbard, which as a nonprofit association and not municipal library must conduct all its own operations (including bookkeeping, payroll, etc.) in addition to significant fundraising, which largely falls to staff and not the board. The Kellogg-Hubbard has usage, visits, and circulation, at about 75% of the level of the Fletcher Free Library in Burlington, which serves a much larger population (42,500), has roughly twice the budget and is administered by the municipal government as a department. Among the sixteen case study libraries in *Common Place*, the Kellogg-Hubbard has the highest patronage on a per capita basis, with only a town-operated library coming close, albeit the larger and better endowed Cary Memorial in Lexington, Massachusetts.[35]

A recent board president, who completed his four-year term in 2019, said the board has considered for some time preparing a strategic plan for the Kellogg-Hubbard, which while not required by the state of Vermont for support, is considered a best practice to follow. One of the Co-Directors will lead this, focusing on both the future role of the institution in Montpelier and lifelong learning. The former president observed the scores of elementary and middle school students that descend on the library each afternoon, as many of their parents (and grandparents) did, reflect the future of the Kellogg-Hubbard. He emphasized the fact that the library is very engrained in the life and even spirit of Montpelier, and whether this continues in the future will depend on whether the board and staff continue to stress community engagement.

# Field Memorial Library

16 Elm Street, Conway, MA

Established: 1901

Benefactor: Marshall Field

Conway is a typical small, rural New England town settled in 1762 on the eastern slopes of the Berkshires in western Massachusetts. Its current population is less than 1,900 and the town has a mean household income of roughly $56,000. The local economy has always been based on agriculture, although its proximity to Deerfield Academy, Amherst College, and other institutions of higher education in the Pioneer Valley have led some in the academic community to reside there. Conway has a single site on the National Register of Historic Places, an 1882 bridge over the Deerfield River. Many residents and visitors would agree, however, that its most notable and beautiful place is the Field Memorial Library, opened in 1901.

Depending upon who you ask, Marshall Field, the founder of Marshall Field's department story and namesake of Conway's library, may not be *the* most respected resident in Conway's history, despite his accomplishments and generosity. That honor may belong to Archibald MacLeish, a noted poet, author, and playwright who served as the Librarian of Congress between 1939 and 1944. Quite the opposite of Field, he was born near Chicago into family made wealthy through founding of another department store, but he came east for his education at Hotchkiss, Yale, and Harvard (read more about Hotchkiss in the Scoville Public Library vignette). MacLeish was a professor at Harvard from 1949 until 1962, then becoming a lecturer the next year at Amherst College for another four years during the height of the 1960s. Shortly after this, he went to work on a musical and asked Bob Dylan to write songs for it.

More importantly for this story, MacLeish was sworn in as the Librarian of Congress in July 1939 by the postmaster of Conway. President Franklin D. Roosevelt's nomination of MacLeish was controversial and the American Library Association (ALA) and some Republican members of Congress opposed the nomination due to perceptions he was "merely" a poet and was sympathetic to communist causes. He had lived in Paris from 1923 to 1928 among the community of literary expatriates including Ernest Hemingway, Gertrude Stein, and John Dos Passos and was openly anti-fascist. He published *Land of the Free* in 1938, a book of poems built around a series of photos taken during the Depression by Dorothea Lange, Walker Evans, and others. The book influenced Steinbeck in writing *The Grapes of Wrath.*

In spite of the ALA's lack of enthusiasm for MacLeish, modern library scientists view his brief leadership of the Library of Congress as enlightened and he has been called "one of the hundred most influential figures in librarianship during the twentieth century." In addition to many management improvements, MacLeish was a strong advocate for the Library of Congress and libraries more generally. He left to work in high levels of the Department of State and War Department during the closing two years of WWII, including helping to establish a new Research and Analysis Branch of the Office of Strategic Services, the Central Intelligence Agency precursor. In spite of this record, he was attacked during the McCarthy period of the late-1940s and 1950s by J. Edgar Hoover and Joseph McCarthy.

As a decades-long resident of Conway, MacLeish not only used the Field Memorial Library but served on its board. Today, the bulk of MacLeish's personal papers and his personal library are down the hill from Conway within the Archibald MacLeish Collection at Greenfield Community College library. It is notable that they were placed there, and not one of the prestigious colleges he taught at, or the Field Memorial Library for that matter. Other smaller collections do exist, however, at a number of colleges and universities including at Amherst and Smith Colleges and the University of Massachusetts, Amherst libraries, as well the Library of Congress.

**Library History:** Marshall Field built the Field Memorial Library in memory of his parents John and Fidelia Field. He was born in Conway in 1834 into a family of subsistence farmers. Field finished his education at a school in the area of town known as Pumpkin Hollow and left the family and farm at age seventeen for what was to become fame and fortune "out West" where he established Marshall Field and Company, the Chicago-based department stores. Historians consider him the tenth wealthiest American of all time, and the wealthiest to have made that fortune in retail. He is widely credited with the creed "the customer is always right." His generosity in Chicago also resulted in the creation of the Field Museum and Library of Natural History and the purchase of land for the University of Chicago campus. The first is considered, along with the American Museum of Natural History in New York City and the Smithsonian Institution's National Museum of Natural History, as among the top museums of their type worldwide. Field once said, however, that the gift that gave him the greatest pleasure was the Field Memorial Library.

While living and working in Chicago, Field returned not infrequently to visit his parents and sister who lived immediately south of Conway in the town of Williamsburg. During a visit in 1899, Field chose the site for the library and selected his architect. The next year a foundation had been created and construction began, with the cornerstone being laid on July, 4 1900. The library's dedication a year later was the largest event ever experienced in Conway, either before or afterwards. Every town resident was invited along with members of the town's diaspora. Some 1,200 people attended. In brief comments, Field stated that he hoped the library would "be a power for good and lasting benefit to this community." Afterwards, guests enjoyed a march, music, and dinner under a huge tent in front of the library's front steps.

Besides funding the design and construction of the library building, Field donated 6,000 books to start the collection. He and later his descendants also endowed its operations. The Field is operated as the town of Conway's public library through a nongovernmental organization overseen by a board of trustees.

**Physical Setting**: Conway is a hill town and its center developed along the banks of the west branch of the South River whose route provided an important early pass through the Berkshires connecting the Pioneer Valley and its Connecticut River with the Hoosic River watershed and the industrial towns of Adams and North Adams.[36] The Conway town center thus takes an east-west linear form along Route 116, but near where the west branch meets the north, the ground flattens out, and there sit the town hall, post office, and the Field Memorial Library.

The building exterior viewed from Conway's main street, Route 116.

The Field was placed with great thought in the most prominent location within Conway at a bend in Route 116 (known in the town as Main Street) at the head of the highway's axis as it heads downhill from the west. The view of the impressive building is stunning. Across Main Street from the building is a small common, and to its left across Elm Street stands town hall.

For the library building, Marshall Field used the best architects and builders his vast wealth could buy. The latter went on to construct the New York City Library, completed in 1911. The architects were the Boston firm of Shepley, Rutan and Coolidge, which had grown out of the well-known practice of Henry Hobson Richardson.[37] They, like him, were known for the popular architectural style in the late-1800s, Romanesque Revival. However, the Field Memorial Library did not follow this style, but rather was designed as low-slung building in the Beaux-Arts style Richardson had studied in Paris and brought to America, which became influential by 1900.

The Field Memorial Library has Palladian influences; today its central dome feature has a green copper patina reminiscent of Thomas Jefferson's Monticello. Marshall Field bequeathed the building first as a memorial to his beloved parents and second for use as a public library for the town's residents. Its appearance leaves no doubt of the structure's primary purpose; a scaled down version would not seem out of place in one of the large urban cemeteries of the day.

The building is built of limestone quarried in Indiana. Its rotunda beneath the copper-clad dome is forty-two feet high, has a diameter of twenty-five feet, and bears a quote from a seventeenth-century English mathematician and theologian, Dr. Isaac Barrow, which reads, "He that loveth a book will never want a faithful friend, a wholesome counsellor (sic), a cheerful companion, an effectual comforter." The stunning interior of the library features Brescia Violet marble from Italy, a spiral staircase, and cast-iron shelving. A vibrantly colored mosaic tile floor lies beneath the overhead dome. The building's perfectly symmetrical layout has reading rooms on both flanks and the stacks to the rear. Both reading rooms have marble fireplaces with a portrait of Marshall Field over one and portraits of his parents over the other. Even today the original card catalogue is still in use; the library does not use computers in any way (nor is there off-street parking for use by library patrons). It remains a historic relic, which is what Marshall Field intended.

**Library Use Today:** The library's use today reflects the nature of the Field Memorial Library's history as first a memorial and secondarily a public library for the town of Conway and the town's demographics. On an average weekly basis less than fifty patrons visit the facility, which has a library director and two assistants. Unlike a number of other libraries in these case studies, the greatest usage is among adults (30–65) and seniors (over 65). This patronage does, however, reflect community demographics. Like many other hill towns in western Massachusetts, the population is aging, as is indeed the case in many communities throughout New England. Given that the onsite book collection is limited, patrons are no doubt attracted by the public computer and Wi-Fi or the few community programs the library offers, such as yoga classes, occasional concerts, and visits by elementary school classes.

Conway has a population of 1,900 residents, the third smallest number among the case studies after Ashaway, Rhode Island, with a population of 1,485, and Lisbon, New Hampshire, with 1,600. The Ashaway Free Library has weekly patronage of approximately 250 users while the Lisbon Public Library has patronage similar to the Field. On an annual basis, the Field usage works out to roughly 1.25 visits per person, with this same figure for all public libraries in Massachusetts during 2017 being 6.06 visits per resident.

Perhaps not surprisingly, leadership of the Field characterizes community support as weak. This honest assessment may reflect the governance and financing of the library, which are inseparable. The library, although public, is a nonprofit NGO run by a trust established by Marshall Field's grandson. There is a five-member board of trustees responsible for oversight of the trust and operation and maintenance of the Field. While the board has delegated the administration of the library to its director, the only paid albeit part-time employee, it sets the vision for the institution, such as it is, and "keeps the lights on." Board members are essentially community volunteers; they receive no compensation, are not elected, and the seats have no term limits. There is little community oversight, although the current board president is a local farmer and small businessman. There is no requirement, as is the case with many boards of NGO public libraries (such as the Bridgton Public Library), that a member be a resident of the town.

The trust established by Marshall Field and formalized by his grandson covers nearly all operating expenses from generated interest. Occasional capital expenditures, such as a new roof, are also covered by the trust. Library leadership estimates that the town of Conway covers roughly five percent of all expenses on an annual basis. This is the lowest level of any public library among the case studies and reflects the library's genesis as a personal memorial made by an individual to his parents, that happens to also function as a public library. This gift, generous as it was, relieved the town of Conway from not only establishing a public library as other small towns were doing, in some cases such as nearby Turners Falls and Athol with support from a Carnegie grant, but also contributing to its operation over the decades that followed. The topic of the local public library rarely comes before the town meeting, nor do town residents appear to have a means to voice interests or concerns to the library board of trustees. It is no wonder that the Field Memorial Library has to be one of just a very few public libraries still using a card catalogue, a quaint remembrance of a bygone era.

The Field Memorial Library Board of Trustees and Director. The photo at the right is of the building exterior.

Due to the size of the bequest and the nature of the trust, the library has never sought other charitable donations from community residents or local foundations, again in contrast to other NGO public libraries operating in New England small towns. For example, the Bridgton Public Library is a nonprofit NGO, yet receives over 40 percent of its budget from the town and other required resources from both a variety of individual and foundation contributions and spirited community fundraising. This is largely lacking in Conway, likely because citizens do not feel a similar degree of ownership. The library does have a small but enthusiastic Friends of the Field Memorial Library group, which conducts limited fundraising through semiannual book sales, community outreach, and some event programming.

**The Future:** The board of trustees says it has a mission statement for the Field, but there is no forward-looking strategic plan as is common in other, even small town, public libraries. Such plans are often required for state certification and support, which in the case of the Field is not considered a requirement. The future vision, such as it is, appears to be continuity and more of the same, which is undoubtedly in line with the terms of the trust and thus the original vision of Marshall Field.

This means in practice that the nearly 2,000 residents of Conway do not have a local modern public library on par with those found in even small towns throughout much of New England. This is not to say they lack access to the same in neighboring larger towns like Northampton and Amherst, where they are allowed book check-out privileges for a small nonresident fee. It is unlikely that town residents would support the cost of establishing a real public library at this point in time, so this model of regional public libraries serving surrounding areas may be the future. This may be a shared future for much of small town and rural America.

# Carnegie Public Library

201 Avenue A, Turners Falls, MA

Established: 1903

Benefactors: Andrew Carnegie and "town fathers"

The Carnegie Public Library in Turners Falls, Massachusetts, is notable in two respects. First, it is located in a village established in 1868 within the town of Montague, a planned industrial community, that sits aside falls in the Connecticut River that provide abundant and inexpensive hydropower tapped through construction of a dam and power canal that generate electricity to this day. Second, a donation from Andrew Carnegie funded the construction of the library building, and it is thus one of thousands of Carnegie libraries built across America during the late 1800s and early 1900s—a story in itself presented below. Montague also has two other smaller branch libraries located in the villages of Millers Falls and Montague Center.

The village, which today has a population of around 4,500 residents and a mean household income of about $55,750, was laid out in a grid pattern with streets named by number and letter. Avenue A, the main street, is a grand tree lined avenue—designed to serve as a mid-1800s village common. The Carnegie is sited on a prominent corner on this avenue, a short walk from the small business district. The library was part and parcel with the development and marketing of a planned community, following in the earlier footsteps of Holyoke, Massachusetts, further down the Connecticut River (see pp. 100–107). Major industries included paper manufacturing and at the time the largest cutlery factory in the world. In the village just south of Turners Falls, the Montague City Rod Company produced three-quarters of all fishing rods in the world between 1900 and 1920. Turners Falls Historic District was listed on the National Registry of Historic Places in 1982.

Turners Falls, like many former industrial mill towns throughout New England, has seen better days. Both in terms of its history and current socioeconomic condition, it is a far cry from the quaint New England village, with a poverty rate of over 25 percent among residents under eighteen years of age. Like many similar small towns across New England it has been buffeted by the opioid epidemic.

**Library History:** The donation agreement from Andrew Carnegie in 1903 specified that Carnegie would provide half the funds required for library building construction, $13,500, and that the town must provide the remaining half through issuing bonds, as well as provide the land. The town select board created a special committee to advance the plans, which included Norman Farwell who was the President of the Crocker Bank in Turners Falls. Entrepreneur Alvah Crocker founded the bank; he led the establishment of Turners Falls as a factory town following a similar successful experience in Lowell, Massachusetts. In is interesting to note that 1903 was the year that Carnegie made the largest number of library grants (203) across America.

**Physical Setting:** Because Turners Falls was not established until the latter half of the 1800s, it did not contain a common like early New England towns and villages. Instead, it had a Main Street—tree-lined Avenue A—and the town provided the library site on a prominent corner of this street. Diagonally across the street lay the main park and the post office. At the other end of the street lay the Crocker Bank and the Shea Theater, established in 1927 during the town's heyday. These local landmarks and the Carnegie Library essentially formed the bookends of the main street. During WWII, the Carnegie Library served as a civil defense center, at which volunteers were trained to spot enemy aircraft. Since then the town established a monument to its sons that fought in foreign wars, which is immediately adjacent to the library. Today, directly opposite the main library entrance lies a strip mall with the area's largest supermarket, hardware store, Salvation Army outlet, and Dollar General store, the latter a sign of the times in many economically distressed New England towns. On the upside, many residents visit the shopping area on a regular basis and the proximity facilitates library visits.

Like nearly all Carnegie libraries, this one was built to standard plans. One special feature noted by the library director are the attractive yellowish bricks used for the exterior walls brought in from a kiln in Ohio. The considerable extra cost for this construction material, covered by the local promoters, was a sign of the building's importance. The main entry, centered in the front façade, leads directly to the librarian's desk. On one side is the children's book room, and to the other is a small multiple-purpose reading room, today equipped with four computers. Behind the librarian are the main book stacks. While the collection onsite is limited, technology allows patrons access to libraries elsewhere in the commonwealth. The upper floor of the building is one large room used around the perimeter for displays of local natural history and historic artifacts. A seating area in the middle is used for community meetings and events such as performances and lectures. Unfortunately, the space is only accessible by the original somewhat narrow staircase. This limits accessibility and community use. A bank across the street has a community space that is ADA compliant.

The entrance to the Carnegie Public Library, on the main street of Turners Falls.

The building has seen little in the way of remodeling or even renovation, with the exception of a new door and ramp in the back to comply with the ADA. It's notable that there is no off-street parking, as most original patrons walked or biked to the library. Some patrons still do, while the majority that drive frequently park across the street at the strip mall. Still, the lack of parking is an impediment to access and use, especially to the elderly of Turners Falls.

**Library Use Today:** The town of Montague runs the Carnegie Library, and it has a staff of three full time and eight part-time staff. The current library director has been at the library for twenty-two years, seventeen years as children's librarian, and also serves as director for the other two town of Montague public library branches. The Friends of the Montague Public Libraries provide volunteer assistance; for example, with book delivery to patrons who are homebound or have physical difficulty accessing the library. The town's annual appropriation for all three libraries is around $400,000 and the commonwealth of Massachusetts provides another $15,000.

In 2018 the collection included a total of 101,000 items, an increase of 5,000 in a decade, and circulation included 19,000 adult books, 14,000 children's books, and 27,000 DVDs. The children's collection centers on books "they want to read," as the library director put it. The popular youth summer reading program, known as A Universe of Stories, includes a Saturday morning book-to-movie viewing and discussion event supported by the Traprock Center for Peace & Justice and the Friends of the Montague Public Libraries. There are also family movies and weekly Lego events. The library is walking distance to schools, and children often come to the library after school to study and socialize on their own. The Carnegie Library's youth program is ranked number two by the commonwealth in towns under a population of 10,000. The library also supports local home-schooling households between the months of September and May.

The library director noted that the community has a high proportion of residents on some form of public assistance, which increasingly requires online interaction, and the library provides help in accessing it. This includes providing both computer and internet connection, as well as help navigating the bureaucratic system. In addition to providing books and DVDs, the Carnegie Library provides an important local space for social interaction among community residents. Turners Falls has no community nor senior centers. Nor does the smaller, more economically distressed village of Millers Falls. The library director noted that the branch library there is "all that is left."

Community support for the Carnegie Public Library is strong, the director noting "the people love us." The town of Montague's financial support for the library system is stable, if not growing. The town can only fund major public facility expenses associated with the schools, firehouses, and the like one at a time, and upgrades to the library building are lower priority. However, the town meeting votes, when required, on extraordinary but noncapital expenses such as major repairs. The Carnegie draws patronage from other Montague villages, the adjacent town of Gill to the north, and even the city of Greenfield, both located just across the Connecticut River.

**The Future:** The library director noted the sense within the town of Montague that within fifteen years of the Carnegie Library's opening, it was too small to meet the needs of the Turners Falls community. This period was, however, during the town's pre-1960s heyday. Today the town's nadir is behind it, with some new blood flowing into the area, and a renovated Shea's Theatre attracting visitors. The director expects patronage to rise perhaps five percent in the coming decade, with circulation of e-books increasing and traditional books decreasing.

The need today is not a larger library, but one that is more accessible. The goal is to address this during the coming fifteen-year period, include adding adjacent parking and an elevator permitting access to all parts of the building. Both requirements acknowledge that the population of Turners Falls, like elsewhere in New England, is aging and that improved accessibility is a prime need.

## Athol Public Library

555 Main Street, Athol, MA

Established: 1914

Benefactors: Andrew Carnegie and L.S. Starrett

Athol is factory mill town located on the Millers River in north-central Massachusetts. The town was founded in 1762 and today has a population of around 11,600 residents and a mean household income of approximately $49,500. Since the late 1890s Athol has been known for the manufacture of precision tools for machinists and tool and die makers. The largest manufacturer, the L.S. Starrett Company, was established in 1881 and today is still the largest employer in the area. The founder, L.S. Starrett, developed and patented the first precision micrometer, and today the company remains a world leader in this niche. Starrett Tools is one of the last companies still producing precision tools in the United States, although it also has production facilities in Germany, the United Kiwgdom, Brazil, China, and several other states.

Other manufacturing in the area has declined, however, and Athol and the neighboring downstream town of Orange are among the most economically depressed in Massachusetts. In the 1980s Athol had one of the state's highest unemployment rates. This decline has a long history and a number of factors associated with it. One is that during the 1930s the development of the huge Quabbin Reservoir in the nearby Swift River valley. The project's aim was to serve the drinking water needs of Boston and surrounding areas, but in doing so Athol's railway link to the city of Springfield, western Massachusetts' commerce hub, had to be abandoned. The impact on local industry in Athol and Orange was devastating. According to the 2000 census, only 17 percent of residents had a college degree. The population peaked in 1955 and declined through the 1970s to a low in 1980 of 10,634 residents. The 2020 census found a stable, albeit aging population.

**Library History:** While the Athol Public Library building was opened in 1918 under the Carnegie library grant program, the library's establishment provides a fascinating example of the interplay between local civil society and business support in both developing the facility and supporting it to this day.

The first library services in Athol were introduced in 1830 by the Athol Social Library and expanded between 1850 and 1860 by the Athol Agricultural and Mechanical Library. In 1878 the Athol Library Association was formed. A few years later the association offered its book collection to the town on the condition that municipal funds be allocated to construct a library building and purchase additional books. The Athol Free Public Library was thus established in 1886 and overseen by a library committee, albeit in a private home and later a barn leased for the purpose. Around 1900 an Athol native, Wilson H. Lee, then a successful printer in New Haven, Connecticut, initiated negotiations with Andrew Carnegie for a building to house the library collection. Carnegie offered $15,000, but the townspeople at the time refused to commit to funding the necessary land. However, an interim location was identified, and the collection was moved to the Academy of Music building in 1903.

Early library postcards.

A decade later, L.S. Starrett generously leased land to the town on Main Street for a building, and Lee restarted negotiations with Carnegie. In 1916 Athol accepted a $22,000 grant from Carnegie and the new library building opened on Main Street. The library was designed by a Boston architect, following a floor plan suggested by Carnegie.

L.S. Starrett covered the extra cost of a hardwood floor, and Lee contributed a large grandfather clock for the main reading room.

**Physical Setting:** The 7,000 square-foot library building is located in a prominent location on Main Street in downtown Athol, immediately adjacent to the town hall, across the street from a large YMCA facility, and a short walk from the Starrett Memorial Methodist Church building, a (former) train station, the L.S. Starrett Company factory just across the Millers River to the north, and the town's main residential area to the southeast. The library was the first Athol town building to have air conditioning, added in 1969, shortly after a major building expansion. The building was made accessible to patrons with disabilities by 1988, pre-dating the ADA by two years.

A library renovation and expansion in 2014 almost tripled the space to approximately 20,000 square feet. The main library entrance was moved off Main Street to the side of the enlarged structure. Upon entering, the new children's area is to the left and several community meeting rooms are to the right. The Friends of the Athol Public Library and the Literacy Volunteers of Orange/Athol, which receives support from the United Way, share one office on a permanent basis. Adjacent to this room is a small space used by the friends for used books sales. An open stairway leads to the upper level of the new addition and the main floor of the original building, which is now a large reading room. To the rear of the enlarged building are the main adult book stacks and an area for teens. The circulation desk, administrative offices, and smaller meeting rooms ring the main space, which is suffused with natural lighting from the huge bank of windows overlooking the river. The meeting rooms are available free of charge to individuals, community groups, and the town itself for meetings, trainings, job fairs, etc. Outside along the river is a small park with a "story walk" for small children, which the children's librarian uses twice a week during good weather.

**Library Use Today:** In 2010 the Athol Public Library conducted a series of focus groups with a variety of stakeholders including staff, board trustees, town board members, and users (especially teens). The main

Part of the Athol Public Library non-book borrowing collection.

findings included acknowledgment of significant community support for the library, but also competition from other community demands and a confirmation that the library is a vibrant essential service used now more than ever. Programming and an impressive young adult program were mentioned as a library strength. In terms of maintaining the current downtown location in the future, participants noted the positive relationships with nearby businesses, ease of access, and a sense of tradition. Needs identified include increased staffing, especially with skill in technology, more space for both the collection and programming, including a separate "noisy" area for teens, more open hours, including evening and weekends (the library is now open for 3.5 hours on Saturday morning and until 8:00 pm one day a week). Specific comments included getting more books in the library rather than through interlibrary lending, the addition of more nonfiction books, and a better-balanced collection of political thought.

Based on the focus group results, the board and library director prepared a five-year plan of programs and services covering the 2011 to 2016 period, using the American Library Association publication *The New Planning for Results: A Streamlined Approach* as the primary tool. The plan included updates every year with an Annual Plan of Action prepared by the board of trustees and library director. The community meetings and five-year plan served as the primary basis for major expansion and renovation of the library. Funding in the amount of $5 million came from the Massachusetts Board of Library Commissioners, which itself used federal sources of support for public libraries. The remaining $3 million for construction was approved in a vote by the town meeting. (Note the contrast with the funding arrangements for the similarly sized Peterborough Public Library renovation and expansion.) The friends and other local sources and foundations raised funding for new equipment, furnishings, and books. The L.S. Starrett Company led with a $100,000 donation, as well as granting both the original land it had leased to the town and the additional land required for the expansion.

The Athol Public Library has a total collection of approximately 50,000 items, in addition to materials throughout the entire Massachusetts public library system. While book circulation has dropped slightly during the past few years, the expansion project increased patronage and today the library sees around 600 users per week. Proportionally, at about 30 percent of all users, children under twelve years are the largest patron group. Teenagers and young adults both comprise approximately 10 percent of users. The former checkout few books but benefit from STEM workshops and other programming. Adults and seniors over sixty-five each comprise about 25 percent.

The number of library employees is currently eight, only three of whom work full-time at 37 hours per week. Salaries are determined by the union contract and the town meeting votes on them annually. The library director is a town employee under contract to the town manager, appointed in accordance with state regulations, but is responsible to the six-member board of trustees elected by town residents every three years. The board maintains institutional memberships for the library in the American Library Association, the Massachusetts Library Association, and the Massachusetts Library Trustees Association. Both the library itself and the active friends of the library association have about twenty volunteers to assist the paid staff.

The library operating budget comes from the town of Athol, with state aid, grants, and interest from several trust fund endowments used for larger acquisitions and projects. Due to budget cutbacks following the 2008–2009 economic downturn, the library struggled to maintain its state certification, which requires among other things for the public library to remain open a minimum of forty hours per week including some evening hours. Ironically, during this difficult period library use surged—increasing 28 percent in one year. Users told library staff they were giving up home internet service and using the facility computers or 24/7 Wi-Fi access. Families recreated and entertained at the library in lieu of vacationing or having a night on the town. During a ten-year period around this time, program attendance nearly doubled to some 7,800 patrons.

A friends of the library group began in 1980 and is still active today. This civil society organization provides about $5,000 per year for programs at the facility like young adult craft workshops and book author visits. Other programs are supported through the Massachusetts Board of Library Commissioners. The library has a Teen Advisory Council involving a young adult librarian to provide a weekly program for young adults. The children's library provides several programs a week for preschool, toddlers, and preteens. The business and career center contain eight public-access computers, obtained through a grant from the Bill & Melinda Gates Foundation. Many Athol residents in outlying areas do not have reliable internet access as broadband and DLS service are not available. Those with only dial-up service frequent the library for downloading large files or to speed up their work process. The library also contains an archives room with over 400 books of local and regional history as well as town directories and reports. In addition, a noted town historian has left his extensive collection to the library in his will.

**The Future:** The Library Director, who has worked at the library for over forty years, and the chair of the board of trustees characterize community support as strong. Reflecting town demographics, the percentage of senior users is high in Athol, and this group includes elderly readers including those in the town's three retirement complexes who are unable to get to the library and to whom books are delivered and returned by volunteers. There is a high demand for book groups and this interest is seen as only likely to grow as the area's population ages. At the same time, in a change from recent years the number of town families with small children is again growing. Additional open hours is at the top of the wish list.

Pocket park outside the Athol Public Library. The L.S. Starrett factory is in the background.

In September 2016, the board of trustees approved a new long-range plan of library programs and services covering the period of 2017 to 2022. The plan was developed following the ALA's *Strategic Planning for Results* publication and with considerable community input obtained through focus group workshops and a survey. Focus group comments included enthusiasm for both current and additional programming and an interest in more intense courses offered through the library and an expression of willingness to pay a fee for these. Related library aspirations included adding more educational programs, especially tech programs for small groups or one-on-one that would fill a need for older adults who do not want to travel to community colleges (the closest being an hour away) or cannot afford the cost. Adults, twenty to thirty years of age without children, is an untapped user group.

The plan focused on making the best use of the larger, renovated library building and contains measurable objectives that staff and the board will continuously monitor and evaluate annually. Based on the results of this assessment, the overall plan's Annual Plan of Action will be adjusted. The plan's new Mission Statement is:

> The Athol Public Library is a welcoming and vital community center where people of all ages and abilities can satisfy their curiosity, become informed, increase their knowledge and skills, connect to the online world, stimulate their imagination and enrich their lives.

The statement covers the broad service areas deemed most important in the planning process, including literacy, pleasure reading, viewing, listening and learning, public internet access and lifelong learning. Actions to meet many of the associated goals and objectives are ongoing, but some are new. For example, establishing a budget line item for acquisition of nontraditional items for lending (e.g., a telescope), establishing outreach services for elderly and disabled patrons, and identifying ethnic groups and languages in the community and begin building a collection, and providing programs to better serve those demands.

## Lisbon Public Library

45 School Street, Lisbon, NH

Established: 1926

Benefactors: Herbert Bigelow Moulton (Parker Young Company)
and Harry Chandler

Lisbon is a small town in north-central New Hampshire, with a population of 1,600 on the Ammonoosuc River, which flows from the western slopes of the nearby White Mountains. Today, the mean household income is around $51,400. The town was established in 1763, named Concord, but went through two other name changes before a new governor in 1824 renamed the town a final time to Lisbon, in recognition of a friend who had been counsel in the Portuguese capital.

Mining and charcoal making were early industries, and the swift water of the river provided power for many mills and factories. By 1920 Lisbon was home to the largest supplier of piano sounding boards in the world—the Parker Young Company—fed by old-growth spruce logs hauled from the slopes of the White Mountains by the largest lumber railroad in all New England. As piano experts and musicians know, the sounding board is the heart of a great piano amplifying the sound of the strings struck by the hammers connected to the keys. The best wood for a sounding board is old-growth spruce due to its high elasticity, resonance, and reverberance. The very best spruce is harvested when the tree's sap is at its lowest content and the wood has a grain of about ten annual growth rings per inch (i.e., it's slow-growing). This is what the best Steinway pianos use, and what Parker Young and the town of Lisbon supplied for years.

**Library History:** While today it's a quiet small town, in its heyday during the 1910s and 1920s Lisbon was a thriving town that boasted a large school, prosperous bank, opera house, orchestra, two dramatic companies, and numerous businesses. During this period the president of Parker Young was Herbert Bigelow Moulton. A hotel he established, now named the Lisbon Inn, is on the National Register of Historic Places. More importantly for our story, Moulton gave land next to his company's factory beside the river and $15,000 to help build the town library in 1926.

Postcard of the newly opened Lisbon Public Library.

He was not, however, the only library benefactor. Its establishment was also made possible by a large donation from Harry Chandler, a local boy "made good" who became the publisher of the *Los Angeles Times* in 1917. Chandler was, however, more than a noted newspaper publisher, he was also a leading civic figure and real estate developer in his adopted city and indeed the entire West. Among the varied public and business ventures that he helped establish during the 1920s and 1930s were the Los Angeles Coliseum (and 1932 Summer Olympics held there), the Hollywood Bowl, the Ahwahnee Hotel in Yosemite National Park, California Institute of Technology in Pasadena, CA., Trans World Airlines (TWA), the Automobile Club of Southern California, and the Pacific Electric Cars that crisscrossed the Los Angeles metropolitan area before the freeways. On the basis of his real estate development holdings and personal ranches, he was the largest private landowner in the United States at one time.

Plaque recognizing the contribution of native son Harry Chandler in establishing the Lisbon Public Library.

**Physical Setting:** Lisbon was established late as a New England village and never had a common. Arguably the most important road in Lisbon, aside from Main Street, the highway connecting Lisbon to neighboring towns that parallels the river, is School Street. The library is on the riverbank on School Street directly across from the Lisbon Town Hall. The building is similar in appearance, layout, and size to the many Carnegie libraries built across America during the prior two decades.

It was constructed by Lawrence Goudie, born in the Shetland Islands in 1855, who came to area to work as a farmhand. He also built the town hall, public school, the main church, and the large New England Wire Company mill building in 1898 upriver from the library. This company, today known as New England Wire Technologies, employs 400 locally, owns subsidiaries in California and Mexico, is the economic lifeblood of the town, and has taken over from the defunct Parker Young Company as a major private-sector partner of the Lisbon Public Library.

**Library Use Today:** The town administers the Lisbon Public Library, which also serves the adjoining small towns of Lyman and Landaff. Both the library director and one part-time assistant are employees of the town of Lisbon. All non-staffing costs are also covered by the town. On a typical weekly basis there are normally around 50 patrons, most visiting weekday afternoons. The library is not open evenings or during the weekend. Children and teens comprised around one-quarter of this number, while seniors over sixty-five years comprise another 25 percent of users. The overall number of patrons has increased slightly in the past decade, although book circulation has declined.

Interior of the Lisbon Public Library. The portrait over the fireplace is library benefactor Herbert Bigelow Moulton, the President of the Parker Young Company.

The library collection comprises nearly 10,000 volumes onsite and access to other books and materials through the state-wide interlibrary loan system. The Lisbon Public Library also belongs to the New Hampshire Audio Book Consortium, which permits downloading of titles to home computers and transfer to MP3 players. The library offers little in the way of community programming, although there is a computer and Wi-Fi available for community use. During the summer holidays, however, there is a popular children's afternoon reading program for the first month of summer featuring stories, crafts, special guests, snacks, and prizes.

Residents elect members of the five-person board of trustees. The current board chair said most members must be "encouraged" to run for positions, and thus many incumbents remain in their seats for two terms, or ten years. There is no library friends group, although staff and board members conduct an annual plant and bake sale every May to help raise funds.

**The Future:** The library building has never been expanded since its completion in 1926, although the library obtained a grant in 2002 for an architect to assess community needs with library and town officials and develop plans to address them. The primary physical improvements noted were lifts at the outer front steps and inside to provide enhanced access and compliance with the 1990 Americans with Disabilities Act. However, the architect retired and only a single blueprint remains in the possession of the town. There is no true sense of the cost today of the desired improvements. This, together with low library patronage and support and overall economic distress of the area, may stymie efforts towards a brighter public library future.

# Munson Memorial Library

1046 South East Street, South Amherst, MA

Established: 1930

Benefactors: Mary Jordan Munson and William H. Atkins

Amherst, Massachusetts, established in 1759, has for years been one of America's premier small college towns, home to Amherst College (founded 1821), Hampshire College, and the University of Massachusetts Amherst—three of the five colleges and universities in the area. The population of Amherst as a whole is around 38,000 residents, but this number swells by another 30,000 or more when the colleges and university are in session. Amherst is a literary town. Emily Dickenson was born and spent her life there, and Robert Frost and Noah Webster also resided in the town, the former while he taught English at Amherst College. The Munson Memorial Library is located in and serves South Amherst, which has a population of approximately 5,000 and a mean household income of about $69,800.

**Library History**: The Munson Memorial Library is special because it serves as the inspiration for this book. It is located on the South Amherst Common, known historically as Fiddler's Green. It serves residents from South Amherst and parts of surrounding towns. Mary Jordan Munson bequeathed funds for the community building in which the library is located in memory of her husband, and William H. Atkins donated the land on the edge of the common.

Like many public free libraries in New England, the Munson was predated by a private subscriber library, known as the South Amherst Library Association, established in South Amherst in 1793, only a few years after the town itself was founded in 1759. The book collection of the original library, like many similar subscription or lending societies, was first located in the home of the church deacon and later the local general store.

Munson Memorial Library, South Amherst, MA.

The Munson family moved to South Amherst in 1881 and built a fine home on Shays Street (named after Daniel Shays, the leader of a rebellion in western Massachusetts in 1786 and 1787 concerning perceived economic injustice), located a short distance from Fiddler's Green. Mary Munson, then a widow, bequeathed $30,000 for "the erection of a library building to be known as The Munson Memorial for the use of the inhabitants of Amherst." Both the Amherst Library Association and the South Amherst Library Association worked to make the bequest a reality. A member of a longstanding and respected South Amherst family, William H. Atkins, donated a building site on the common next door to the South Congregational Church, first established on the commons in 1824 as a community meeting house and only in 1915 formally as a church. The Munson was run by the South Amherst Library Association until 1952 when it became a department of the town of Amherst.

Significantly, the Munson Memorial was and still is considered a community center with a library room, a large hall used for frequent dances and other social functions, and two kindergarten rooms. At one time there was a small playground on the site. During a brief period in the early 1950s, the books were removed to the main Jones Library in downtown Amherst. Today the Munson continues to serve residents of South Amherst as one of two branches of the Jones Library system. In addition to a collection of some 8,500 titles, it provides a public meeting room and hall (reserved through the town's website) and serves as a polling place during elections like many libraries around America.

The Munson community hall is used for social functions including as an official voter polling center at election times.

**The Physical Setting:** Fiddler's Green was historically the center of South Amherst life. Major roads converge upon the common including those leading to Amherst proper, the railway station, and the area's major thoroughfare linking Boston and the Connecticut River. The Munson Memorial is situated on the southeastern corner of the common, next to the South Congregational Church. Nearby, in the southwestern corner, was the general store, which also served for decades as the post office. Today it is a private home. A watering tub for horses still stands in front, now filled with flowers. On the southern edge of the common lay houses occupied by the church deacon and the Munson librarian. Further north on the western side of the common was the first public grade school in South Amherst, opened in 1902, which is used today for students with special needs. At the far north end of the common stood between 1838 and 1914 the town's "poor farm" for the indigent, and the asylum on the opposing side of the common. (It is interesting to note that these needed, but undesirable, public facilities were placed on the common, but at the far end from the church and library.) Today the annual Amherst-wide Fourth of July parade and picnic, as well as other episodic community events, take place on the common in front of the library.

**Library Use Today:** The Munson has its regular collection of titles with many other books quickly available from the town's main facility, the Jones Library, or other public library systems throughout the commonwealth. On a monthly basis use ranges widely; for example, in 2018 use went from a low of 1,200 people in June to a high of 2,400 in August (this figure includes users there for community activities and events besides library use). Book circulation currently runs in the range of 30,000 per year, down from an all-time high of 58,000. The librarian estimates that a decade ago patronage was 30 to 40 percent higher, and of current users only 20 percent are under the age of thirty years, with 50 percent of users being between the ages of thirty and sixty-five years. These figures reflect the aging population of the surrounding area. Among users older than sixty-five, some reside in a nearby retirement community. The library takes book orders by phone and volunteers deliver and return books from the elderly residents. Library programs include a long-running book club and a popular weekly visit by a young IT expert to assist community members. The Munson is open twenty-four hours per week with a staff of four part-time town staff and four to five regular volunteers.

Activities that take place in the community portions of the library building, which include a hall and stage, and meetings rooms reserved with the town, include kids' movement and dance classes, adult yoga, and tai chi classes. Besides use for voting, the Munson building has also seen use for social events including weddings.

The interior of the Munson is warm and inviting.

The Munson's annual operating budget is between $90,000 and $100,000, some of which comes from the commonwealth of Massachusetts. The annual budget for new purchases is under $15,000, which is in addition to the operations budget which covers staff, utilities, and routine building maintenance. In addition, there are occasional capital expenditure funds made available from the town, commonwealth, and federal government. For example, there was a major $300,000 building renovation in 1988. The system-wide friends of the library does ad hoc fundraising, as does the Munson-specific board of trustees. The three-member board was required as a condition of the original bequest and is semi-independent from the town, although the town manager appoints the members for three-year terms.

**The Future**: Although she characterizes community support as moderate to strong, the librarian believes that the recent decline in library use will continue without action. She identified suggested steps to stabilize if not increase usage including staying open more hours, some during evenings and more on the weekend, and greater use of the building's community spaces for new programs. She cited using the high-tech AV equipment in the meeting hall for communal educational/learning events such as talks and group learning communities. The librarian noted, however, that Amherst is unique given all the local colleges with such facilities, which are generally open to the public at large.

The town of Amherst public library system recently conducted a community survey that will feed into long-range plans for the two Jones Library branches, including the Munson. The survey included questions on use of each branch, programming and services, collections and technology, customer service, library (branch) strengths and weaknesses, and personnel.

# SECTION III:

## Future of the Public Library

"To Restore Civil Society, Start with the Library," a September 8, 2018 opinion piece in the *New York Times*, began by asking if the public library was obsolete. It is a reasonable question given changes in technology, lifestyles, and perhaps values reflected in civil society. Is the declining use, at least in terms of book borrowing, seen in many public libraries an unstoppable trend? Is the public library yet another social institution afflicted with the bowling alone syndrome highlighted by Putnam nearly twenty-five years ago?

In speculating about the future of nearly anything it is important to set the context of the possible future. It helps to consider both the past and present, the first for precedence and the second as a starting point.

While the first public libraries in America, including those in New England featured in this book, were established over a series of decades the epicenter of this period occurred during the Progressive Era, roughly a period of two decades spanning between 1895 and 1915. This era was preceded by the Gilded Age and was followed by the Roaring Twenties/Jazz Age.[38] Historians of the era note that Progressives focused their attentions on towns and cities, although many hailed from rural areas of America. Noted achievements of urban reformers during the period were good governance, clean water supplies, more efficient transportation, and public libraries.

This book is not the place for a thorough lesson of American history of 125 years ago, but some reflection on the transition between the nineteenth and twentieth centuries is useful because it helps in thinking about the future. The social, political, and economic reforms associated with the Progressive movement were a reaction to the rapid and profound changes taking place in America during the Gilded Age at the end of the 1800s, including technological innovations such as electricity and the motor vehicle, as well as industrialization, urbanization, massive immigration, and rising economic inequality.

The values and morals of the Progressive Era were also a counter to those of the Gilded Age, which have been characterized as social Darwinism or survival of the fittest. In reaction, Americans led by the Progressives came around by the turn of the century to the belief that "society needed to be democratized to ensure everyone a decent chance for life, liberty and the pursuit of happiness."[39] What's more, "Progressive intellectuals articulated a broader yearning among many Americans for community values of small-town life, nostalgia provoked by the materialism, individualism and 'bigness' of the new America."[40] This general social philosophy served as the foundation for many civil society efforts associated with social capital and social institutions including the public library.[41] There are parallels today with this earlier time of rapid and often disruptive change. Indeed, Putnam hinted at this when describing the Progressive Era.

> By the turn of the century, complacency bred of technological prowess was succeeded by dissatisfaction, civic inventiveness and organized reform efforts fueled by a blend of discontent and hopefulness. Over the succeeding decade this flourishing, multifaceted movement—spouting from the seeds sown in the Gilded Age and dependent on the tendrils of social connectedness—would produce the powerful era of reform in American history.[42]

He concluded by noting that we "need an era of civic inventiveness to create a renewed set of institutions and channels for a reinvigorated civic life that will fit the way we have come to live... The specific reforms of the Progressive Era are no longer appropriate for our time, but the practical, enthusiastic idealism of that era—and its achievements—should inspire us." Putnam wrote these words nearly two decades ago, but they still ring true today. The public library came into its own during that earlier period of reform and once again it can be at the forefront of the type of renewed social institutions America needs in the future.

Social scientists have not coined a widely used term for the current era, and as in the past, it may fall to historians to do so. Regardless, the effects of the rapid technological and scientific advances of the past quarter century are not dissimilar to those experienced at the end of the nineteenth century. The current era also has similarities to the Gilded Age in terms of socioeconomic values and beliefs. Some would characterize capitalism, as practiced today, as not dissimilar to the social Darwinism of that earlier age. Nor are the consequences on social and economic equality dissimilar between then and now. The impact of immigration and concerns about jobs and assimilation also resonate in both periods. Recall that the surge in public library establishment came during the height of the Progressive Era, which also brought with it a boom in voluntary civic associations, which peaked in 1910, but served as the foundation of social capital growth for another half century. The question, then, is whether there will be a counter movement to the recent period as the Progressive Era was to the Gilded Age. If so, what does that mean for social institutions and in particular the public library?

As the preceding material in this book has shown, in general and in terms of specific public libraries throughout their modern history in America, libraries as institutions have been intrinsically linked to literacy; that is, reading and writing. The Latin root of the word, lit, means letter, read, or word, but in modern usage the meaning of literacy has come to denote competence or knowledge in a specific area such as information technology or medieval history. The future of public libraries ties to this broader meaning and the recognition that books are no longer the sole or even primary means of developing literacy in a topic. The Cary Memorial Library, for example, is increasingly using experiential learning programs for this purpose. The increased presence of tech-robotics makerspace labs in public libraries, like the McArthur in Biddeford, exemplifies this wave of the future for this type of programming. Overall, the goal of the Peterborough Town Library, to "champion literacy in all forms," frames the issue well.

The American public appears to agree with this emphasis on broadened literacy. The Pew Research Center's Internet & American Life Project, with support from the Bill & Melinda Gates Foundation, periodically surveys Americans concerning how they value public libraries in their communities. In 2013 the survey[43] found the following: 95 percent of Americans ages sixteen and older agreed that the materials and resources available at public libraries play an important role in giving everyone a chance to succeed.

The same proportion of respondents said that public libraries are important because they promote literacy and a love of reading.

- 94 percent said that having a public library improves the quality of life in a community.
- Interestingly, only 81 percent of respondents said they had ever used a library in their lifetime.
- 81 percent said that public libraries provide many services people would have a hard time finding elsewhere.
- Nearly 70 percent of Americans agreed "I like to learn a lot" describes them "very well."
- Libraries are particularly valued by those who are unemployed, searching for a job, living with a disability, retired, or lacking home internet access.[44]
- Only 54 percent of Americans have used a library in the past twelve months (although 61 percent said they have a library card), and 52 percent of Americans said that people do not need public libraries as much as they used to because they can find more information on their own.

In 2016, the survey found that a downward trend in public library visits had steadied and that many Americans had high expectations for what their libraries should offer. When asked to think about the thing libraries could do in the future, notable numbers of Americans responded in a way that could be summarized in one phrase, as Pew's report puts it, "Yes, please." Eighty percent of those surveyed believe that public libraries should offer programs that teach people digital skills, a clear example of public support for strengthening literacy in forms other than reading.[45] Other examples noted in the case studies include spoken and written language skills, entrepreneurialism, and even handling difficult discussions better. As these examples illustrate, citizens, with guidance from library staff, are best placed to determine what types of improved literacy are most needed in their communities.

Aside from improving literacy through their collections, and by libraries of things; and programs, including experiential learning, future libraries can also better serve their communities in terms of being a welcoming place. Sixty-nine percent of survey respondents felt that libraries contribute "a lot" to their communities in terms of providing a safe place for people to hang out—the type of informal gathering spot or non-home or work "third place" that sociologist Ray Oldenburg termed back in 1989 as instrumental in building association between citizens and thus social capital. Evidence from many of the New England case study libraries indicates that the public would like to see more community spaces added to public libraries, albeit not necessarily at the expense of room for books.

Perhaps a model to consider is the Progressive Era's Chautauqua movement, which combined learning, largely from lectures, and entertainment. The Chautauqua grew out of the earlier lyceum movement, which began during the first half of the 1800s. The two differ in that the lyceum emphasized educational purpose, while the Chautauqua tended more towards entertainment, albeit generally around serious topics. Today's remaining athenaeums still embrace this combination, such as the Redwood Library and Athenaeum in Newport, Rhode Island, which is basically a subscription library with a lyceum program.

While the term placemaking is often associated with the planning, design, and management of outdoor public spaces, the concept also has applicability to the interiors of social institutions, to use Eric Klinenberg's term, such as libraries. Indeed, placemaking creates and maintains sought-after public third places.[46] The Project for Public Spaces has offered placemaking advice on how public libraries can serve as community anchors and places for bring people together to engage and associate with each other.[47] This menu of library-as-place attributes includes:

- a broad mix of community services
- dialogue and exchange among patrons
- combination of local history and global information
- serving as a resource for local business and entrepreneurs
- multiuse community spaces for both formal and informal gatherings
- physical and visual linkages to the surrounding townscape
- the creation and thoughtful management of sub-spaces within and around the library offering multiple uses, attractions, and amenities.

What this boils down to is a shift from the library as nearly exclusively a repository for books and place for quiet reading, to more of a people-focused place offering a greater variety of public uses, experiences, and opportunities. The design for the expansion and renovation of the Peterborough Town Library follows much of this formula (see pgs. 67–77).

Were public libraries to become community anchors, would they then provide a fertile habitat for the regrowth of civic engagement, which has declined across America in the last half century? It must be said that no social institution directly addresses the primary causes of disengagement identified by Putnam, namely generational change, work habits, sprawl (and associated commuting), and television (now with the addition of the internet). Putnam attributed at least half of the decline to the first factor, and at that time the major shift was the waning of the silent generation born before 1935. Today the most salient factor is engagement from the millennial generation. There are some hopeful signs, such as measurable increase in volunteerism and even voting among millennials. Notably, as the Pew survey results indicate, this age group reports using public libraries (including websites) the most—53 percent of millennials versus 36 percent of the silent generation. Pew research attributes this interest to nontraditional (i.e., nonbook) uses, especially oriented around technology.

In terms of civic engagement, the volunteer rate among millennials in 2015 was 22 percent, compared to 29 percent for Gen X, the highest of all age groups. Eighty-four percent of millennials reported making a charitable donation in 2014. In contrast, Putnam found the youngest age group in his 1990s research (Gen X) the most civilly disengaged at the time. Perhaps most encouraging from the Pew surveys involving millennials is their sense of optimism. In 2015, 49 percent felt the country's best years were ahead, compared to 42 percent among Gen X, 44 percent among baby boomers, and only 39 percent of the silent generation. In any event, public libraries do appear to have a renewed draw on younger Americans.

Putnam mapped social capital by state, and the best scores on his index were found in the states of the northern plains, the Pacific Northwest, New England, and in Utah. The lowest scores clustered in the South.[48] This research has not been precisely replicated to update his seminal findings, but the federal government's Corporation for National and Community Service is currently using a similar approach to assess social capital. The results of the survey field work are not yet available, but other data related to civic engagement and social capital is of interest. For example, the millennial volunteer rate by state both aligns and contrasts with Putnam's social capital map. Utah, South Dakota, and Minnesota recently ranked highest in volunteerism, and in the past they were highest for social capital. Louisiana remains at the bottom in both assessments. Within New England, Maine ranked eleventh in the country for millennial volunteerism, with the other New England states not faring so well. Washington, DC, had the third highest rate of millennial volunteerism.

Appendix III contains facts concerning libraries in the six states in New England and three other states relevant to social well-being research as a comparison. The information provided includes state-level data from the Institute of Museum and Library Services (IMLS) FY 2019 Public Library Survey, the Gallup-Sharecare's 2017 and 2020 Well-Being Indices, the 2017 and 2019 Opportunity Indices scores and Putnam's 2000 social capital index.[49] Following Putnam and other researchers that have followed him, the level of social capital plays a key role in overall well-being and opportunity.

The Well-Being Index includes measures pertaining to five interrelated elements that make up well-being: (1) sense of purpose, (2) social relationships, (3) financial security, (4) relationship to community, and (5) physical health. The first, second, and fourth elements tie directly to social capital. The survey research began in 2008, and in 2017 for the first time no state improved its well-being index score; while the majority remained stable, a record twenty-one states declined from the previous year. The previous record, a decline in fifteen states, happened in 2009 reflecting the impact of the 2008 "Great Recession."

The Opportunity Index measures four dimensions: economy, education, community, and health. Three are closely related to the Well-Being Index. Within community, the percentage of adults over eighteen years who volunteer is the most relevant factor to social capital development and maintenance measured. As we have seen above, this rate is up among millennials. While the index does not break out age groups within the adult population, Vermont, which topped the community category nationally within the overall index, had a volunteerism rate 33 percent of all adults, eight percentage points higher than the national average.

The results from all indices are set against the Centers for Disease Control (CDC) 2018 announcement that for an unprecedented third year, the average life expectancy in America declined.

Both the Well-Being Index and Opportunity Index results closely track Putnam's social capital index scores of twenty years ago, both reflecting the similarities in the measures and long-term continuity in social capital/well-being strengths and weaknesses.[50] Many states changed positions within the middle ranks of the Well-Being Index, but the same states remained at the top and bottom. As the table indicates, in 2017 Vermont (tied South Dakota) had the highest Well-Being score of 64.1, while in comparison, West Virginia and Louisiana had scores at the bottom with 58.8 and 58.9 respectively. This was the first time that Vermont occupied the top position. This was reportedly due to scoring highest in the element of community, which is broadly defined as "liking where you live, feeling safe and having pride in your community." It should be said that Vermont has the smallest population of the states examined and is predominately rural, which Putnam associated with higher level of social capital.[51] In 2020 Vermont's score and national ranking dropped but Massachusetts rose to the top and Rhode Island improved dramatically. Ohio, which scores very well in terms of public library financial support and usage, received a Well-Being ranking in the middle of the pack.

In terms of the Opportunity Index, overall New England had, on average, the highest scores in America in both years. Vermont again tops the list, and Massachusetts is in the top five nationally. Ohio's ranking is again in the lower half of all U.S. states, and again Louisiana and West Virginia rank near the bottom of the fifty states.

Turning now to the 2019 IMLS library data, not surprisingly Vermont again tops the list and West Virginia and Louisiana are at the bottom. While, given its smaller population, Vermont does not have the highest number of library systems (generally per town or municipality), it does have the lowest number of people per system, with just over 4,000, compared with nearly 30,000 in Rhode Island and over 70,000 in Louisiana.[52] Within its library collections Vermont has the second highest number of books per resident, second only to Maine, which has nearly double the number of Louisiana. Aside from books, public libraries also offer programs and here again Vermont does best with nearly 53 programs per 1,000 residents, notably higher than West Virginia, Louisiana, and even Ohio which has the highest library expenditure per capita. Finally, public libraries offer free computers, Wi-Fi, and internet access to patrons. Again, Vermont tops the list with 8.87 internet access points per 5,000 residents. Only Maine, another rural state, comes close with 7.46. West Virginia, poor and rural with many residents lacking home computers and internet access, only has 3.73 access points per 5,000 of its residents.

In terms of financial support, the figures are interesting. Vermont spent around $47 per resident, in the middle of the group, while Louisiana expended a bit more and Ohio, topping all states, expended over $68 per capita. At the extremes, West Virginia spent a bit less than $21 per resident and, within New England, Connecticut expended nearly $64. These figures reflect no doubt the economic conditions in the states and, therefore, government budgets, but it also appears that Ohio is not seeing the benefit of its relatively high expenditures on libraries. West Virginia's low expenditure is likely one factor for its very low numbers of public library programs and internet access.

In terms of library use, the figures are what one would expect. Vermont has the second highest number of visits per person, just under Ohio, and West Virginia the lowest reflecting no doubt its low expenditures. Library use is also lower in Louisiana. Interestingly, within New England, New Hampshire and Rhode Island have similar population sizes, although the latter is more urban as reflected in its library locations. Visits per person in the two states are in the middle of the pack and nearly identical.

There has been no complicated statistical analysis conducted to determine whether the clear correlation between the Well-Being and Opportunity scores and public library support/use data in in states like Vermont or West Virginia reflects a causal relationship. Does a healthy public library system contribute to well-being and opportunity, or does the well-being of residents and/or other opportunities (e.g., education levels) in a community or state contribute to a good library system? The IMLS research (see below) seems to establish a sound correlation between public library support and use with community health, particularly in rural areas.

Based on the case study research in New England contained in *Common Place* one could conclude there is a relationship, and it works both ways. While neither wellbeing nor opportunity was measured by Gallup-Sharecare in any location examined in the case studies except for Norwich, Connecticut, which was selected for this precise reason, the differences in qualitatively assessed library health, community well-being, and opportunity are clear when comparing places like the similarly sized small towns of Ashaway, Rhode Island, (higher) and Lisbon, New Hampshire, (lower), or within Massachusetts in Athol (higher) and Turners Falls (lower)—all former mill towns, the latter two located just a few miles from each other.[53]

What explains the differences? New research may help answer this question. The IMLS announced in August 2018 that was starting a multi-year study, Understanding the Social Wellbeing Impacts of the Nation's Libraries and Museums, which was released to the public in October 2021.[54] The thesis behind this research is that public libraries have the potential to serve as community anchor institutions. This term has recently come into use to denote institutions such as universities and hospitals that are anchored in a community (i.e., they can't easily be physically relocated) and help drive economic development even in distressed areas. Yale University in downtown New Haven or the University of Southern California in central Los Angeles are prime examples. IMLS believes public libraries in some cases play the same role, albeit primarily in terms of fostering social wellbeing.[55] The case studies found that the McArthur Library in Biddeford, the Otis Library in Norwich, the Athol Public Library, and the Guilford Free Library all function as anchor institutions in their respective communities, which range from small cities and towns to a very rural village.

The IMLS study created indices which compared library presence and utilization, and several wellbeing measures at the level of over 3,000 U.S. counties. Libraries were grouped into four categories by the population and location of the communities served, these being: rural; micropolitan; suburban; and urban. (The library case studies in *Common Place* fall into the first two categories.) Based on the presence and usage measures, libraries were placed in 10 deciles, 10 being the highest level. The wellbeing measures were grouped into three baskets: economic and human capital; social connection; and health and security.

The study reported in detail on the human capital measure of school effectiveness and the health measure of "community health." The correlation between high decile libraries and school effectiveness was present but modest, but for community health it is "dramatic."[56] The most consistent set of relationships between the library index, school effectiveness and community health are found in rural areas. This IMLS finding supports the thesis expressed in *Common Place* that the importance of public libraries for strengthening community wellbeing is particularly valuable in underserved rural areas.

The other generational question linking libraries and civic engagement is whether, as the baby boomers continue to age, they will repeat the silent generation's diminished use of the public library, or will the library of the future see a U-shaped curve with use increasing from a low point during middle age. Ways to increase such use are discussed below, but here it is important to note that as a social institution, libraries have the potential to engage both ends of the adult population. For this engagement to occur among either group there must, of course, be attractions to each. Some of these will differ, for example around use of technology, but a common denominator is also possible and falls under the general rubric of lifelong learning.

The typical library user lifecycle involves first visiting the local public library as a toddler to have children's books read by family members. Getting one's own library card. Using school libraries through primary, secondary, and perhaps higher education. Followed by a hiatus in library use. Taking one's own children for early introduction to reading and books. Using the library occasionally as an adult, perhaps as part of a book club. Declining use in senior years often due to accessibility challenges. This may—no, should—change, as America's population grows older and lifespans lengthen. Libraries have the potential to become a foundation of both individual and community lifelong learning efforts.

In 2016, Pew looked in greater detail at the question of public libraries and learning and found that over 75 percent of Americans felt libraries serve the learning and educational needs of their communities "very well" or "pretty well." At the same time, many did not know that libraries offer learning-related programs and materials such as ebooks, career and job resources, and high school certificate courses. Significantly, but not surprisingly, women, blacks, Hispanics, those in lower-income households, and those aged thirty and older rated public library performance more highly in this regard. Another Pew survey conducted about the same time found that 76 percent of adults felt the label "life-long learner" applied "very well" to them. Ninety-seven percent of those who used a public library in the past twelve months say the same term applies "very" or "pretty" well. While the two surveys were separate, it appears there is a correlation between the strong interest in lifelong learning and library use. The Peterborough, Scoville, and Cary libraries showed this correlation.

This finding is somewhat at odds with other Pew findings that among the four major adult age groups surveyed, public library use was highest for millennials and Gen X, at 53 percent and 45 percent, and lowest among baby boomers and the silent generation, at 43 percent and 36 percent respectively. Across all age groups, women are 15 percent more likely than men to have used a public library in the past year, possibly in part due to their mothering role of taking small children to the library for books and other programming. The high percentage of millennials' library use is likely tied to another finding: parents of young children are 11 percentage points more likely to have used a library during the year.

The data indicates that among those adults at a stage of life where lifelong learning has additional meaning (i.e., senior citizens) library use tapers off. Less use by the oldest Americans is likely related to accessibility issues, because even though use of bookmobiles were covered in the survey, these are less likely to visit widely dispersed seniors. Some case study libraries, such as in Biddeford, provide individual book delivery and return, but this service is costly in rural areas and difficult to scale. Also, exacerbating this decreased use is the fact that many in the silent generation are less likely to appreciate or be able to use the new tech platforms public libraries increasingly deploy.

The catch is that many libraries offer IT classes and individual support, often geared towards seniors, but one needs to get to the library to take advantage of them.

If as noted earlier over 75 percent of American adults consider themselves practitioners of lifelong learning, what does the term mean in practice, and how can the public library better contribute to the process? To begin with, here is a definition of the term: Learning that extends beyond childhood or the classroom but takes place throughout life and in a range of situations involving formal or experiential (tacit) learning. The pursuit of knowledge either for professional or personal reasons. The former is instrumental and is especially associated with millennials, while the latter, expressive, links with senior citizens; however, neither is exclusive. Today's environment prompts lifelong learning—a world of increasingly rapid change where the half-life of a particular skill or knowledge is shrinking, and a surfeit of available information and knowledge brought about by "big data" and the internet. Advances in information technologies facilitate lifelong learning. For many, the expressive form, or learning for its own sake, is simply a pleasurable pastime. In a knowledge economy and aging society, lifelong learning is a distinct advantage.

A senior patron of the Munson Memorial Library receiving IT coaching from a volunteer.

Among an aging population, such learning can strengthen engagement with others and lessen social isolation (e.g., through participation in study circles), improve one's quality of life and perhaps even forestall mental decline by exercising an aging brain (Grady, 2016). At a minimum research shows that older adults' participation in nonformal lifelong learning is positively associated with their psychological well-being (Narushima, et. al, 2016). This is especially true for a portion of life commonly referred to as the third age, adults in their 60s, 70s, and 80s.

Lifelong learning linked to professional or vocational knowledge and skills is thus attractive to younger individuals as work requirements evolve, as increasingly will be the case. For a variety of reasons learning for the sake of learning is also attractive to many including older adults in their third age.

There is also a third justification for emphasizing lifelong learning in the future and considering the role the public library may play. In his recent book, *21 Lessons for the 21st Century*, the noted historian Yuval Noah Harari considers the consequences of the rise of artificial intelligence (AI) and automation on the workforce and the possibility of massive redundancies at nearly all levels, "No remaining human job will ever be safe from the threat of future automation, because machine learning and robotics will continue to improve" (Harari, 30). In the chapter of the book titled, "Work: When you Grow Up, You Might Have a Job," he asks if mankind will see the rise of a new "useless class... leading to social and political upheavals that no existing ideology knows how to handle."

In his *Washington Post* review of Harari's book, the scholar Moises Naim highlights this provocative idea and notes that in Harari's judgement it will become necessary if not inevitable for governments to step in and support the "useless class" with various forms of public aid, including a guaranteed income to cover basic needs. More importantly, however, Harari notes that such economic support is not alone sufficient. Providing a meaningful existence for those with little or no work over a lifetime will be a crucial yet monumental task. Along with some form of a guaranteed minimum income, if not the more controversial universal basic income, such public aid might also include a computer with high-speed internet connection, a public library card and accessible public library.

In his book Harari cites the example, imperfect as it is, of some ultra-Orthodox Jewish men in Israel who never work but instead study religious scriptures and perform rituals. In other words, they spend their adult lives learning and serving in a manner valued by their particular community. This is possible because the Israeli government provides a stipend, or minimum income, to support this lifestyle. Some other Israelis resent this arrangement, but few characterize these ultra-Orthodox as a "useless class." The label useless doesn't apply to any post-work socioeconomic classes in in America; but what would be a more appropriate descriptor? Although a euphemism, I will use "learning class" as the term to describe not just Harari's hypothetical displaced group, but if we are honest about it, a growing number of Americans today. Learning and the public library together provide a potent combination that can help to address the issue Harari notes, "In the lives of people, the quest for meaning and community might eclipse the quest for a job" (Harari, 43). Whether or not that proves true it is certain that meaning and community are important in human lives, as the Well-Being Index indeed measures.[57]

While Americans said they needed public libraries less to find information they need, instead relying increasingly on the internet, the Pew survey found that libraries can help people decide what information they can trust. Many American struggle with how to discern reliable information found on the internet. In the era of "fake news" they want help in knowing trusted sources and the facts about both current events and information in general. In 2016, 37 percent of Americans felt that public libraries contribute "a lot" in this regard, a thirteen-point increase from just one year earlier. Seventy-eight percent of Americans felt public libraries provide the type of help needed to find information that is "trustworthy and reliable." Millennials, whose internet use is by far the highest of any age group, feel most strongly (87 percent versus 68 percent of the silent generation), as do Hispanics (again, 87 percent) about this fundamental characteristic of the public library.

However, over 60 percent of Americans feel that training on how to use online resources to find trustworthy information would help them "a lot" or "some" in making decisions. Blacks, Hispanics, and women feel especially strongly about this, as do those without a high school diploma. This type of training is not something many libraries currently offer for online resources, although it comes as second nature for information resources within the library itself as it is the traditional role of the reference librarian.

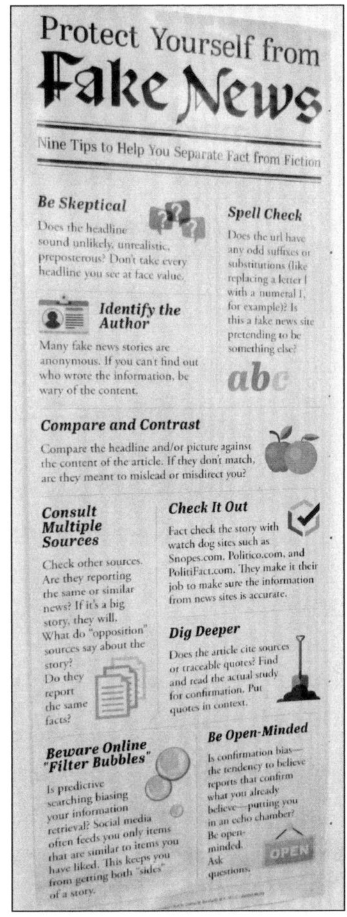

A poster containing information on "fake news" on the wall of the Ashaway Free Library.

The future of the public library is promising. A diverse cross-section of Americans, and notably younger generations, value many of the services these community institutions provide, even if book borrowing continues its decline. Like other public institutions, however, libraries must change with the times in reflection of national trends such as an aging population and changing work demands, as well as community interests and needs. Like any change this may be difficult for some traditionalists to accept. Promoting "literacy for all" may be the best commonly accepted goal if it is approached in a broad sense. In any event, public libraries must continue to reflect their civil society roots and the civic values that animated their creation in New England over 200 years ago. In this way they can continue to contribute to individual and community well-being and opportunity, and even the practice of democracy in America.

# Epilogue

SINCE THE RESEARCH AND PUBLIC LIBRARY CASE STUDY FIELDWORK for *Common Place* began in late 2018 there have been significant developments which have affected libraries, as well as national socio-political changes which are reflected by important themes in the book. The COVID-19 pandemic which began in the spring of 2020 has affected nearly every aspect of life in America including the accessibility to and use of public institutions such as libraries. The sixteen case study libraries adapted to the new realities, as did libraries across the country. In-person service was curtailed for a period, and provision of online services and programming increased. Like with other parts of our personal and professional lives, increased online resources will remain even as public libraries have re-opened and in-person visits increase to pre-pandemic levels.

During the preparation of the book America elected a new President, in the midst of the pandemic and all its associated social and economic consequences — which continue to evolve until this day. Public libraries were not an explicit target of COVID relief funds such as the American Rescue Plan and the infrastructure bill, both of which were enacted, or the proposed "Build Back Better" legislation. Nevertheless, libraries will benefit indirectly such as through the greater access to broadband, including in underserved rural areas, where public libraries provide community residents with public internet access and sometimes loan devices to utilize it. One case study library, for example, received American Rescue Plan funds to provide an additional 20 hotspots for its Wi-Fi lending program.

Aside from these large legislative packages, in early 2021 members of Congress introduced the "Build America's Libraries Act," which if passed would provide $5 billion to repair, modernize and construct library facilities in underserved and marginalized communities. Funds would flow to the IMLS which would then grant all fifty states a minimum allotment of $10,000,000 each. There are similar bills in both the Senate and House and as of August 2021 nearly 150 bipartisan co-sponsors. Unfortunately, at this point passage of the Act appears uncertain.

The new administration is also more supportive of public libraries than its predecessor. Funding for the federal government's Institute for Museum and Library Services (IMLS) is likely to increase relative to the amounts requested in recent annual budget appropriations. Any such funding would ultimately reach local public libraries in the form of grants or in-kind support. Such assistance would offer support to the recent IMLS's own research findings, discussed in *Common Place,* which show a link between better and more used public libraries and improved community health, and the correlation between public libraries and community wellbeing and economic opportunity highlighted in this book.

Unfortunately, one thing that has not changed since late 2018 is the state of the socio-political arena in America. Many Americans still suffer alienation and many informed observers continue to agree that the republic has fractured in significant ways. The pandemic may well have exacerbated these conditions. Causes and results of fracturing often involve diverse information sources and the associated issue of "fake news," which if anything seems to be on the rise.

In February 2022 a guest essay titled "The Battle for the Soul of the Library" appeared in the *New York Times.* The essay, written by Dr. Stanley Kurtz, a senior fellow at the Ethics and Public Policy Center, a conservative think tank, addressed the growing debate about what books students should have access to in their school libraries. The author cites the ALA's Library Bill of Rights in which librarians pledge to "provide materials and information presenting all points of view on current and historical issues." This stance is known as "neutrality," which Kurtz applauds, noting that "the library should remain sacred ground—a neutral sphere above the fray—precisely because libraries leaven and inform the fray itself." The essay concludes by noting that supporting—be they public or school—library neutrality is in everyone's interest and therefore should be both promoted and protected

Indeed, as *Common Place* has noted, public libraries continue to provide their patrons with sources of information which are identified and offered in an unbiased manner. While there may be an alternative set of "facts" involving nearly any issue, the historic role of the reference librarian is to provide access to the array of information for the user to consider in forming their own opinion or belief. This neutral role/function of the public library must continue, be it involving books or online sources of information.

Wherever they are located public libraries are an invaluable part of America's social infrastructure and are widely supported regardless of one's education, economic circumstances or political orientation. In this sense they are important "mediating institutions" and can in the future increasingly serve as places to strengthen social capital which bridges within and across physical and interest communities in America. As much as he valued books and libraries as a key means to increase knowledge, Benjamin Franklin would no doubt as well approve of this important societal role for the institution.[58]

# Appendix I
# Timeline of Public Library History

**Public Library History in New England**

1650 | 1700 | 1750 | 1800 | 1850 | 1900 | 1950 | 2000

- Harvard University Library
- New Hampshire State Library - 1st in U.S.
- Franklin's "Lending Library" in Philadelphia
- Redwood Library and Athenaeum in Newport, RI
- Franklin Public Library (MA)
- Library of Congress (Philadelphia-Washington, D.C.)
- Scoville Memorial Library (Salisbury, CT)
- Massachusetts State Library established
- Cary Memorial Library (Lexington, MA)
- Peterborough Town Library (NH)
- NH Legislature passes law to permit tax support
- Otis Library (Norwich, CT)
- MA passes law to permit tax support
- Boston Public Library
- ME passes law to permit tax support
- McArthur Public Library (Biddeford, ME)
- VT passes law to permit tax support
- Holyoke Public Library (MA)
- Ashaway Free Library (RI)
- American Library Association (ALA) founded
- ALA chartered in Massachusetts
- 1st State Library Association (NH)
- Massachusetts creates Free Public Library Commission
- Guilford Free Library (VT)
- CT passes law to permit tax support
- Bridgton Public Library (ME)
- Kellogg-Hubbard Library (Montpelier, VT)
- Field Memorial Library (Conway, MA)
- Carnegie Public Library (Turners Falls, MA)
- Athol Public Library (MA)
- Lisbon Public Library (NH)
- Munson Memorial Library (Amherst, MA)

## Appendix II: Further Case Study Information

| TOWN | INCOME | ST | POP. | EST'B. | LIBRARY NAME | ADDRESS | EST'B. | FOUNDER/BENEFACTOR | LEGAL |
|---|---|---|---|---|---|---|---|---|---|
| Franklin, MA | $123,208 | MA | 33,000 | 1778 | **Franklin Public Library** | 118 Main Street | 1790 | Benjamin Franklin | TOWN |
| Salisbury, CT | $103,134 | CT | 4,000 | 1741 | **Scoville Memorial Library** | 38 Main Street | 1803 | Jonathan Scoville | NGO |
| Lexington, MA | $189,916 | MA | 34,000 | 1713 | **Cary Memorial Library** | 1874 Mass. Ave | 1827 | Town Meeting Maria; Hastings Cary | TOWN |
| Peterborough, NH | $ 72,993 | NH | 6,300 | 1760 | **Peterborough Town Library** | 2 Concord Street | 1833 | Rev. Abiel Abbot | TOWN |
| Norwich, CT | $ 65,335 | CT | 39,500 | 1659 | **Otis Library** | 261 Main Street | 1850 | Joseph Otis | NGO |
| Biddeford, ME | $ 57,583 | ME | 21,250 | 1653 | **McArthur Public Library** | 270 Main Street | 1863 | Robert McArthur | NGO |
| Ashaway, RI | $ 92,202 | RI | 1,485 | 1757 | **Ashaway Free Library** | 15 Knight Street | 1871 | Hannah Cundall and Sylvia Salisbury | NGO |
| Holyoke, MA | $ 52,568 | MA | 40,000 | 1850 | **Holyoke Public Library** | 250 Chestnut Street | 1886 | J.P. Morgan; William Skinner | NGO |
| Guilford, VT | $ 57,674 | VT | 2,000 | 1791 | **Guilford Free Library** | 4024 Guilford Ctr. Rd. | 1890 | Cynthia King (books) | TOWN |
| Bridgton, ME | $ 46,933 | ME | 5,200 | 1794 | **Bridgton Public Library** | 1 Church Street | 1895 | Dr. Nathan J. Dalton | NGO |
| Montpelier, VT | $ 68,125 | VT | 7,500 | 1818 | **Kellogg-Hubbard Library** | 135 Main Street | 1896 | Martin & Fanny Kellogg; John E. Hubbard | NGO |
| Conway, MA | $ 56,094 | MA | 1,900 | 1767 | **Field Memorial Library** | 16 Elm Street | 1901 | Marshall Field | NGO |
| Turners Falls, MA | $ 55,749 | MA | 4,500 | 1868 | **Carnegie Public Library** | 201 Avenue A | 1903 | Andrew Carnegie; Town Select Board | TOWN |
| Athol, MA | $ 49,492 | MA | 11,500 | 1762 | **Athol Public Library** | 555 Main Street | 1914 | Carnegie and Starrett | TOWN |
| Lisbon, NH | $ 51,411 | NH | 1,600 | 1824 | **Lisbon Public Library** | 45 School Street | 1926 | Harry Chandler (LA Times) | TOWN |
| Amherst. MA | $ 69,775 | MA | 38,500 | 1759 | **Munson Memorial Library** | 1046 S. East St. | 1930 | Mary Munson and William Atkins | TOWN |

## Appendix III: Public Libraries and Social Capital, Well-being and Opportunity

| STATE | Well-Being | | Opportunity | | Putnam | Population | Systems | % Non | % Rural | Persons per | Books per | Exp. per | Visits per | Programs | Internet |
|---|---|---|---|---|---|---|---|---|---|---|---|---|---|---|---|
| | Score (Rank) | | Score (Rank) | | Rank | | | profit | or Town | system | capita | capita | capita | per 1000 | per 5000 |
| | 2017 | 2020 | 2017 | 2019 | 2000 | | | | | | | | | | |
| **New England** | | | | | | | | | | | | | | | |
| Connecticut | 61.7 (20) | 66.0 (10) | 58.7 (8) | 58.9 (10) | 17 | 4,145,970 | 180 | 42.8 | 30 | 23,033 | 4.01 | $63.69 | 5.77 | 34.66 | 6.36 |
| Maine | 61.6 (24) | 57 (29) | 57.9 (12) | 58.0 (11) | 13 | 1,278,373 | 228 | 61 | 87 | 5,607 | 4.86 | $42.03 | 5.44 | 40.75 | 7.46 |
| Massachusetts | 62.5 (8) | 71 (1) | 60.5 (4) | 60.9 (4) | 18 | 6,719,857 | 367 | 6.5 | 29 | 18,310 | 4.25 | $50.91 | 5.75 | 27.19 | 5.14 |
| New Hampshire | 62.8 (5) | 61 (16) | 59.7 (7) | 59.2 (8) | 8 | 1,443,798 | 220 | 3.2 | 81 | 6,562 | 4.11 | $48.75 | 5.08 | 42.42 | 5.59 |
| Rhode Island | 60.5 (41) | 64 (12) | 54.5 (24) | 56.3 (20) | 24 | 1,431,901 | 48 | 54.2 | 18 | 29,831 | 2.99 | $51.31 | 4.91 | 33.87 | 6.93 |
| Vermont | 64.1 (1) | 59 (22) | 63.3 (1) | 63.0 (2) | 3 | 659,471 | 162 | 35.8 | 95 | 4,071 | 4.74 | $47.48 | 5.89 | 52.91 | 8.87 |
| | | | | | | | | | | | | | | | |
| **Other** | | | | | | | | | | | | | | | |
| Ohio | N/A | N/A (31) | N/A | 49.9 (36) | 29 | 11,502,000 | 251 | 7.6 | N/A | 45,824 | 3.30 | $68.08 | 5.91 | 26.82 | 6.02 |
| Louisiana | 58.9 (49) | 53 (43) | 42.4 (50) | 43.7 (50) | 45 | 4,703,681 | 67 | 0 | 61 | 70,204 | 2.48 | $49.16 | 3.46 | 20.43 | 6.38 |
| West Virginia | 58.8 (50) | 50 (47) | 44.8 (47) | 45.3 (48) | 42 | 1,852,994 | 97 | 0 | 75 | 19,103 | 2.56 | $20.71 | 2.52 | 15.04 | 3.73 |
| | | | | | | | | | | | | | | | |
| Note: Public library statistics are from the FY 2019 IMLS national survey | | | | | | | | | | | | | | | |

## Appendix IV
## Andrew Carnegie and the Carnegie Libraries

As noted in *Common Place*, if there is a father of the public library in America, the title should go to Benjamin Franklin. The single name most associated with libraries in the minds of many Americans is, however, Andrew Carnegie, one of the so-called robber barons and the foremost Glided Age philanthropist. This association is due to the network of nearly 1,690 Carnegie libraries established across America by this industrialist and investor between about 1880 and 1920. The estimated cost at the time was between $40 and $41 million, or roughly $1.2 billion in today's dollars. Carnegie's stated goal was to give away all his wealth during his lifetime. He failed in this aspect of his storied, controversial career; however, public libraries received the majority of Carnegie's philanthropic giving to what he considered worthy causes.

Andrew Carnegie was born in 1835 in a small industrial town in Scotland and immigrated to America with his parents and brother in 1847 to Allegheny, a suburb of Pittsburgh. His parents were both literate and believed in the value of education for their two sons. His father helped create a tradesmen's subscription library in their hometown and imbued a love of reading in Andrew, who received formal education only between the ages of eight and twelve.

Upon arrival in the Pittsburgh area the Carnegie family originally struggled, and it soon became apparent that the household's welfare would depend largely on Andrew (his brother, Tom, was eight years younger). Although Andrew immediately went to work, his "book learning" was just to begin. Within a year of arrival in America, he was working as telegraph messenger boy and taking advantage of the offer of a local businessman, Colonel James Anderson, to open his personal library on Saturdays for young workers like Andrew to borrow books. Carnegie later said that Anderson's act had opened the windows through which the light of knowledge streamed. Carnegie never forgot that opportunity as he became the epitome of America's self-made man.

Carnegie's rise and wealth coincided with the Industrial Revolution based on technological advances like the telegraph, railroads, use of petroleum for fuel, and steel making. He was involved with them all. Broadly speaking, reformers in the Progressive Era, which began in the 1890s saw public libraries as a source of information about an increasingly complex world and a means to assist millions of immigrants to succeed in America. Free public libraries also provided a wholesome alternative to vices such as drinking and gambling. Carnegie wasn't a leading Progressive, although in an early 1885 interview with *The New York Times* he was asked by the reporter if he was a socialist. He responded, "I believe socialism is the grandest theory ever presented, and I am sure some day it will rule the world. Then men will be content to work for the general welfare and share their riches with their neighbors" (Nasaw, 257).

Around this time both Carnegie's brother, to whom he was close, and his beloved mother passed away. He also decided to finally get married at age fifty. Carnegie might have had what is considered today a midlife crisis. In any event, he began to think seriously about philanthropy and his legacy and, in so doing, provided an example for the charitable organization, the Giving Pledge, founded in 2010 by Bill and Melinda Gates and Warren Buffet.

In 1881, a few months after funding the construction of a public library (the first) in the Carnegie family's ancestral hometown of Dunfermline, Scotland, during an 800-mile long coach trip through Great Britain, Carnegie decided to establish a reading room at a steel mill he owned in Braddock, Pennsylvania, near Pittsburgh. He was not the first factory owner to have the idea to encourage workers to read books, either in Pennsylvania or New England. In 1879 an employee library was established at an iron plant in Johnstown, Pennsylvania, and the public libraries described in the Norwich, Connecticut (1850), Biddeford, Maine (1863), Ashaway, Rhode Island (1871), and Holyoke, Massachusetts (1886), case studies all involved similar employer-supported libraries, which predated Carnegie's efforts. A labor historian who studied these developments during this period wrote that such efforts were "seldom purely philanthropic gestures. Employers who financed [worker] libraries ... looked upon their expenditures as investments in a more efficient as well as a more conservative working class" (Nasaw, 212). This may have been true in many cases, but not Andrew Carnegie. Carnegie seems to have truly believed in the intrinsic moral value of supporting self-improvement.

After 1875 many types of corporate welfare programs and facilities became more common and having himself benefited from Colonel Anderson's private library some thirty-five years earlier, Carnegie soon led the movement with public libraries. The facility in Braddock finally opened in 1889, having transformed from a simple reading room on the factory floor to a social center consisting of a public library, swimming pool, public baths, bowling alleys, art gallery, gymnasium, and billiard hall. Carnegie knew that public libraries and associated facilities should benefit not only the workers themselves, but their families and indeed the community as a whole.

Between 1886 and 1896 Carnegie funded similar community centers in six communities across America, including Pittsburgh. In 1889 he wrote an essay, "The Gospel of Wealth," which laid out his views on wealth and philanthropy. In a follow-up essay, "The Best Fields for Philanthropy," he included seven areas: universities, libraries, medical centers, public parks, meeting and concert halls, public baths, and churches. He pointed out that a library was the best possible gift for a community since it gave people the opportunity to improve themselves.

In the midst of this period union workers at Carnegie's Homestead steel plant outside Pittsburgh went on strike in July 1892. Carnegie was in Scotland at the time and his second in command, Henry Clay Frick, called in the Pinkerton detective agency to protect the property and enforce a lockout of the union strikers while negotiations were underway. Violence erupted, however, and there were a number of deaths and injuries. The incident forever stained Carnegie's reputation, ultimately earning him the epithet of robber baron, although this placed him in the company of another public library supporter, J.P. Morgan (see Holyoke case study). *The St. Louis Post-Dispatch* wrote at the time, "Ten thousand 'Carnegie Public Libraries' would not compensate for the direct and indirect evils resulting from the Homestead strike" (National Park Service, 3).

After 1896, Carnegie scaled up his support of public libraries, in what he termed the "wholesale" phase. The focus was on simpler facilities (i.e., just libraries) in smaller communities with less access to cultural institutions. In even those cases, the Carnegie libraries were the only large public building and they became hubs for social activities. Locations in forty-six states benefitted from the program. Over half were grants for less than $10,000 (Carnegie based the grant size on a rough basis of two dollars per community resident), with the condition that the community must provide the land and an annual allocation of 10 percent of the grant for operations and maintenance. In this way Carnegie intentionally required that benefiting residents and their politicians were invested in the project. Many communities could or would not abide by these terms, at least initially (see case of Athol, Massachusetts). To assist smaller communities, state library commissions often explained the procedures for obtaining grants (Kevane, 8). At its peak in 1903, Carnegie made over 200 community grants. Carnegie also supported the establishment of public libraries across Britain and Ireland, Commonwealth countries, and isolated island nations such as the Seychelles, Mauritius, and Fiji.

A cut-out of Andrew Carnegie (right) in the community hall of the Athol (MA) Public Library, built in 1918 with his support. The figure on the left is Wilson H. Lee, who led the city's negotiations with Carnegie.

Shortly before he passed away in 1919 at the age of eighty-four, Andrew Carnegie halted his support of library building construction. In 1916 he had an economics professor visit some one hundred of the existing libraries and prepare a report on their social significance, effectiveness, and financial condition. The report concluded that to be truly effective, the libraries needed trained personnel who would foster active community institutions as well as appreciation for reading and books. The Carnegie Corporation of New York (the foundation Andrew Carnegie established to continue his philanthropy after his death) subsequently began to support training and education programs for librarians, an early contribution to the library sciences.

This important lesson learned resonates until this day, as reflected in an October 2019 opinion piece in *The New York Times* entitled, "In the Land of Self-Defeat." The piece involves a controversy about a public library in a small town in rural Arkansas, which had constructed a new state of the art library facility, but then had some residents oppose offering the library director a reasonable salary. The writer quoted one dissenting resident, reflecting the views of others, who commented on Facebook, "I've never understood why a librarian needs a four-year degree. We were taught [the] Dewey decimal system in grade school. Never sounded like anything too tough." The standard, if not a requirement, in several states in New England and much of the nation is for the library director to have a master's degree in library science. Andrew Carnegie would have approved.

## Notes

1 Wiegand's 2015 book contains a very useful introduction citing why "Americans love their public libraries." Rather than repeat the quotes from well-known figures and research findings here in the Introduction, I simply commend them to the reader.

2 This was the reason the Young Men's Christian Association (YMCA) established many social libraries as part of their broader programs, particularly in cities with perceived higher levels of vice (Wiegand, 23–24).

3 Wiegand cites mercantile libraries as somewhat performing this function, but employers did not support these self-help associations. These libraries did, however, serve as an inspiration for Andrew Carnegie's massive support of the public library system across America, as his father benefitted from them in Scotland before immigrating to America (23).

4 The State Librarian of Connecticut uses this phrasing of the concept (author interview, April 24, 2019).

5 The term coined by Eric Klinenberg in his book, Palaces for People, for public libraries, parks, and other "shared spaces."

6 Walter Isaacson's biography, Benjamin Franklin: An American Life, describes well Franklin's motivation for establishing the Library Company which thrives to this day.

7 The Scoville Memorial Library case study documents one instance when a book seller and publisher helped to establish a public library.

8 Three types of libraries are excluded from these numbers: private libraries held for the owner's use; elementary and secondary school libraries; and Sunday school libraries. Other church libraries are, however, included in the figures.

9 Early public libraries in Massachusetts included Arlington (1837), Fall River (1837), Lowell (1844), Orange (1846), and Concord (1855).

10 The U.S. Copyright Law, first passed by Congress in 1790, requires that two copies of any copyrighted material be deposited in the Library.

11 When interest in or support of a social library waned books often passed to the town and became part of a public library collection.

12 For whatever the reasons, women and their civil society organizations had an extraordinary impact on the growth of public libraries across America. One source claimed that by the 1930s "75 percent of the public libraries in this country owed their origins to women's clubs" (Kevane, 9). Five out of the 16 libraries featured in this book were founded based primarily on the efforts and support of individual women.

13 In New Hampshire alone, the towns of Rindge, Wentworth, Fitzwilliam, Amherst, and Kingston sited their public libraries on the common.

14 One purpose for which Americans combine he noted was to "distribute books," likely a reference to lending societies and/or public libraries. At the state level he focused his study of democracy in America on the Commonwealth of Massachusetts and thus may have heard of the earliest public libraries in Franklin and Lexington, the latter founded only four years before his visit in 1831 (Tocqueville, 513).

15 In contrast, the percent of NGO-run public libraries in neighboring New Hampshire is very low. In the early 1930s one researcher estimated that 15–20 percent of all public libraries in cities of more than 30,000 people were NGO-run. The proportion in smaller communities was likely to have been if anything higher (Kevane, 7).

16 The organization was founded by over one hundred librarians from around America at the Centennial Exhibition in Philadelphia. The ALA was chartered three years later in, appropriately enough, Massachusetts.

17 There are still private, members-only libraries in existence, mostly athenaeums in cities, but these are rare (found mostly in New England) and are never confused by citizens or the state with public libraries. However, the public libraries in Pittsfield and Westfield, Massachusetts, were formerly athenaeums.

18 This is a central thesis explored in Yuval Levin's 2016 book, *The Fractured Republic.* Putnam offers an interesting response in his latest book, *The Upswing,* focusing on the Progressive Era (see Chapter 8, endnote 16).

19 This individual hails from Connecticut, lives there today, and is very familiar with public libraries in New England.

20 Rev. Emmons, a 1767 Yale graduate, was an influential theologian in New England for half a century. During his time in Franklin he became a chief proponent of what was then know as the New Divinity. He was also a renowned patriot during the War of Independence. That his position on the use of Benjamin Franklin's book donation was over-ruled by the Franklin town meeting is no small thing.

21 The Town of Wayland, MA began operating its free public library the year before, through taxation and before the Commonwealth passed enabling legislation to do so.

22 It is not clear the town had the legal authority to do this, as the enabling legislation was not passed in Massachusetts until 1852.

23 The study defines purpose as "liking what you do each day and being motivated to achieve your goals" and community as "liking where you live, feeling safe, and having pride in your community."

24 Like Biddeford, Maine, by 1900 one in three residents were of French or French Canadian descent.

25 William Skinner was born in England in 1824 and arrived in America before he reached the age of twenty. He moved his successful silk thread and fabric company to Holyoke. Within ten years it had become the largest producer of

silk satin linings in the world. Unlike Andrew Carnegie, J.P. Morgan gave little to philanthropic causes and even less to public libraries. He made an exception in this case apparently because his father, Junius Spencer Morgan (1813–1890), was born in Holyoke. Besides this donation, both Morgans gave in 1890 towards construction of the Free Library in Hartford, Connecticut, where J.P was born in 1837.

26 Unfortunately, when the building was renovated the stack wing could not be brought into code compliance, and it was demolished and replaced. The glass flooring tiles were salvaged by the library and are still available for purchase by collectors (including the author). The new wing contains the new main entrance on Chestnut Street, reference area, and children's room. Across the street are library parking lots, a Masonic Temple and church, and boarded up townhouses.

27 Visitors using the community room for programs may not be counted since they do not enter the library.

28 In 2018, these individuals donated nearly 2,100 hours of effort assisting the summer reading program, conducting research, shelving books, and many other tasks.

29 The Princes were one of the first households in the entire town; it was first settled three years earlier by Michah Rice.

30 Established following fundraising by the local Women's Christian Temperance Union.

31 Harlan was born in Kentucky in a prominent family and supported slavery during the Civil War, but later changed his views and became a strong supporter of civil rights. In the infamous 1896 case, Plessy v. Ferguson, which upheld southern segregation, he was the lone dissenter on the court.

32 It is notable that Montpelier's population grew over 50 percent between 1890 and 1900.

33 Free To All: The Kellogg-Hubbard Library's First 100 Years, pg. 4

34 As early as 1900, the Kellogg-Hubbard created small circulating libraries in surrounding towns.

35 The Cary is the sixth most-used library in Massachusetts, following Boston, Cambridge, Brookline, Newton, and Worcester—all of which are operated by their respective local governments.

36 Unlike all the other major rivers in southern New England that flow north to south and drain into the Atlantic at Long Island Sound, the Hoosic flows north into Vermont before turning west and joining the Hudson River. In the shadow of Mount Greylock, the highest point in the Berkshires, low hills separate the Hoosic watershed from that of the Housatonic River near the small town of Dalton. It is here that Crane Paper has produced United States and many other currencies around the world since 1879. While currency manufacturing has largely moved to plants elsewhere, Crane Paper remains today the sole source of United States dollars.

37 Shepley, Rutan and Coolidge along with Fredrick Law Omstead designed the main quad at Stanford University, South Station in Boston, university libraries at

Brown and the University of Chicago, and public libraries in Chicago and New London, Connecticut.

38 Like any social or historic demarcation, this division of years is not strict as aspects of the Progressive movement for which the era is named had antecedents during the Gilded Age. Likewise, features of the era mingled with those of the period that followed it. It is important to note that throughout history many eras reflect a counterreaction to the preceding period, and the Progressive Era is a prime example.

39 Quandt, 44–45

40 Putnam, 378 (citation of "Putnam" refers to *Bowling Alone* unless otherwise noted)

41 The term social capital was first used by a Progressive Era educator, L.J. Hanifan, expounding the value of community centers, including public libraries.

42 Putnam, 382. Also see Putnam's most recent book, *The Upswing*, which covers the Progressive Era extensively.

43 57 percent of respondents lived in a small city, town, or rural area.

44 An emerging public library service is a 24/7 Wi-Fi connection, available even after hours in the parking lot.

45 At the same time, only 24 percent of respondents supported the idea of moving books and stacks in order to make way for community and tech-oriented spaces; 31 percent disagreed with the idea.

46 Most of the third place hangouts highlighted by Oldenburg were in fact private business establishments, such as coffee shops, bars, and even plant nurseries. If designed and operated with care, sections of both public parks and libraries can also serve as third places.

47 https://www.pps.org/article/libraryattributes

48 See Figure 80, Social Capital in the American States, *Bowling Alone*, pg. 293.

49 Gallup's 2018 Wellbeing Index results show a reordering of state ranking. Hawaii, Wyoming and Alaska ranked highest, while Vermont and South Dakota fell to seventh and ninth places. West Virginia remains at the bottom, while Louisiana rose somewhat to forty-third place. The 2019 Opportunity Index scores are the latest available.

50 Interestingly, Putnam scored neither Hawaii nor Alaska.

51 Putnam's social capital index, composed of 14 indicators, rankings placed North Dakota, South Dakota and Vermont at the top of the state list. Much of the data was sourced from the DDB Needham survey archives. One survey question asked respondents if they "Go to a public library."

52 Public library support, coverage and use has been historically low in southern states such as Louisiana. In 1870 the region accounted for nearly a third of the U.S. population but accounted for only 3 percent of its public libraries (Kevane, 3).

53 The community data for the Opportunity Index is only available at the state level.

54 The research was initiated under IMLS's flagship Community Catalyst Initiative. https://www.imls.gov/issues/national-initiatives/community-catalyst-initiative

55 This is also a premise made by Eric Klinenberg in *Palaces for People* although he does not use the term, opting instead for the broader term social institutions.

56 See Figure 6 on page 42 of the study.

57 The index contains five essential elements of well-being. The first is purpose, which is defined as "liking what you do each day and being motivated to achieve your goals." Another is community, which Gallup defines as "liking where you live, feeling safe and having pride in your community."

58 In *Bowling Alone* Putnam notes that such a role has old roots, citing words expressed at the 1829 opening of a community lyceum in Massachusetts (Putnam, 23).

## Bibliography

Atkins, William H. *Leave the Light Burning: South Amherst, Massachusetts 1871-1952*. Amherst, MA. Marjorie Atkins Elliott, 1973.

Bobinski, George. *Carnegie Libraries*. American Library Assoc. 1969.

Bouthillette, Emma R. *A Brief History of Biddeford*. The History Press. Charlestown, SC. 2017.

Brechin, Gray. Indestructible by Reason of Beauty: The Beaumanence of a Public Library Building. http://graybrechin.net/_docs/books/Indestructible-by-Reason-of-Beauty-Gray-Brechin.pdf

Carney, Timothy P. *Alienated America: Why Some Places Thrive While Others Collapse*. HarperCollins. New York. 2019.

Cass, Oren. *The Once and Future Worker: A Vision for the Renewal of Work in America*. Encounter Books. New York/London. 2018.

Dahl, Robert A. *On Democracy*. Yale University Press. New Haven, CT. 1998.

Dawson, Robert. *The Public Library: A Photographic Essay*. Princeton Architectural Press. New York. 2008.

Deneen, Patrick J. *Why Liberalism Failed*. Yale University Press. New Haven, CT. 2018.

Dickerson, Doris M. and Cliff McCarthy. *Images of America—Belchertown*. Arcadia. Charleston, SC. 1998.

Ditzion, Sidney H. *Arsenals of a Democratic Culture: A Social History of the American Public Library Movement in New England and the Middle States from 1850 to 1900*. American Library Association. Chicago. 1947.

Eliot, Samuel Atkins (Ed.). *Biographical History of Massachusetts: Biographies and Autobiographies of the Leading Men in the State*. Massachusetts Biographical Society. Boston. 1906. Vols. 2 and 5.

Elliott, Marjorie A. (Ed.) *North of Norwottuck: A Sampler of South Amherst, Mass*. F. Irvine and Marjorie Elliott. Madison, Wis. 1985.

Garmer, Amy K. *Rising to the Challenge: Re-Envisioning Public Libraries.* Aspen Institute. Washington, D.C. 2014.

Grady, Denise. *Exercising an Aging Brain.* The New York Times. Retirement, March 7, 2012.

Harari, Yuval Noah. *21 Lessons for the 21st Century*. Spiegel & Grau. New York. 2018.

Institute of Museum and Library Services. *Public Libraries Survey, FY 2015-2016*. Washington, D.C. https://www.imls.gov/research-evaluation/data-collection/public-libraries-survey

Institute of Museum and Library Services. *Understanding the Social Wellbeing Impacts of the Nation's Libraries and Museums.* Washington, D.C. October 2021. https://www.imls.gov/sites/default/files/2021-10/swi-report.pdf

Isaacson, Walter. *Benjamin Franklin: An American Life*. Simon & Schuster Paperbacks. New York. 2004.

Jones, Theodore. *Carnegie Libraries Across America: A Public Legacy.* John Wiley & Sons. New York. 1997.

Kevane, Michael and William A. Sundstrom. *The Development of Public Libraries in the United States, 1870–1930: A Quantitative Assessment*. Information & Culture: A Journal of History, 49(2), 2014.

Klinenberg, Eric. *Palaces for People: How Social Infrastructure Can Help Fight Inequality, Polarization and the Decline of Civic Life*. Crown. New York, 2018.

Klinenburg, Eric. *To Restore Civil Society, Start with the Library*. The New York Times. Opinion, September 8, 2018.

Levin, Yuval. *The Fractured Republic*. Basic Books. New York. 2016.

Manheimer, Ronald J. *Lifelong Learning in Aging Societies: Emerging Paradigms*. https://cpb-us-w2.wpmucdn.com/sites.udel.edu/dist/4/2685/files/2016/02/ORG-01-Lifelong-Learning-in-Aging-Societies-26p33vt.pdf

McMullen, H. *American Libraries Before 1876*. Greenwood Press. Westport, CT, 2000.

Naim, Moises. *Worried fake news spells our doom? Humanity has always lived with it.* Outlook Review. Washington Post. October 26, 2018.

Narushima, Miya, Jian Liu and Naomi Diestelkamp. *Lifelong learning in active ageing discourse: its conserving effect on wellbeing, health and vulnerability*. Cambridge University Press, 2016. (published online 2016 Nov 21 by the U.S. National Institute of Health https://www.ncbi.nim.nih.gov/pmc/articles/PMC5848758/)

Nasaw, David. *Andrew Carnegie*. Penguin Books. New York, 2007.

National Park Service. *Carnegie Libraries: The Future Made Bright*. https://www.nps.gov/nr/twhp/wwwlps/lessons/50carnegie/50carnegie.htm

Norton, Michael H. and Emily Dowdall. *Strengthening Networks, Sparking Change: Museums and Libraries as Community Catalysts*. Institute of Museums and Library Services. Washington, D.C. 2016

Oldenburg, Ray. *Celebrating the Third Place: Inspiring Stories about the "Great Little Places" at the Heart of Our Communities*. Marlowe & Company. New York, 2001.

Orlean, Susan. *The Library Book*. Simon & Schuster. New York, 2018.

Peters, John A. and Nina C. Santaro. *A History of America's First Public Library at Franklin, Massachusetts 1790-1990*. Franklin Public Library Bicentennial Commission. 1990. (Unpublished monograph).

Peterborough, NH. *History of the Peterborough Town Library* (monograph). Undated.

Putnam, Robert D. *Bowling Alone: The Collapse and Revival of American Community*. Simon & Shuster. New York, 2000. (pgs. 192, 201, 213, 218, 231, 318, 337,342, 357, 374, 382)

Putnam, Robert D. and Lewis M. Feldstein. *Better Together: Restoring the American Community*. Simon & Schuster Paperbacks. New York, 2003.

Putnam, Robert D. with Shaylyn Romney Garrett. *The Upswing: How America Came Together a Century Ago and How We Can Do It Again*. Simon & Shuster. New York, 2020.

Quandt, Jean B. *From the Small Town to the Great Community: The Social Thought of Progressive Intellectuals*. Rutgers University Press. New Brunswick, NJ. 1970.

Rand, Frank Prentice. *The Jones Library in Amherst: 1919–1969*. Amherst, MA. The Jones Library, Inc. 1969.

Raine, Lee. *Libraries and Learning*. Pew Research Center. April 2016 http://www.pewinternet.org/2016/04/07/libraries-and-learning

Scott, Kyle J. *Images of America—Montague: Labor and Leisure*. Arcadia. Charleston, SC. 2005.

Shera, Jesse H. *Foundations of the Public Library: The Origins of the Public Library Movement in New England, 1629–1855*. University of Chicago Press. Chicago, 1949.

Talcott, Martha T. *Athol Public Library 1882–1972: 90 Years of Service*. The Transcript Press. Athol, MA. 1974.

Tocqueville, Alexis de. Translated by George Lawrence. Edited by J.P. Mayer. *Democracy in America*. Harper & Row. New York, 1966.

Wiegand, Wayne A. *Part of our Lives: A People's History of the American Public Library*. Oxford University Press. Oxford/New York, 2015.

## Name Index

# Acknowledgments

Many people must be acknowledged for assisting me with *Common Place*, beginning with the directors of the public libraries highlighted in the Section II Case Studies. At the time of the field research these individuals include: Sue Hugus (South Amherst); Carol Baldwin (Conway); Corinne Chronopoulos (Peterborough); Felicia Oti (Franklin); Claudia Cayne (Salisbury); Carolyn Brennan (Montpelier); Linda Hickman (Turners Falls); Heather Field (Ashaway); Karla Houston (Lisbon); Jean Shaughnessy (Athol); Catherine Wilken (Guilford); Amy Stone (Bridgton); Maria Pagan (Holyoke); Jeff Cabral (Biddeford); Koren Stembridge (Lexington); and Robert Farewell (Norwich). All of these individuals hosted me at their libraries and provided invaluable support in the preparation of the case studies.

I also benefited from discussions with the State Librarians of Vermont, Jason Broughton, and Connecticut, Kendall F. Wiggin, who helped provide a bigger picture of the public library system within their respective states. The theme in *Common Place* of the relationship between public libraries and wellbeing coincided with research on this topic conducted by the federal government's Institute for Museum and Library Services (IMLS). Thanks go out to Robin L. Dale, IMLS Deputy Director for Libraries, Marvin D. Carr, IMLS Senior Advisor, who guided the research and Michael H. Norton, Chief Policy Analyst at the Reinvestment Fund, which conducted the research work.

During the early research for the project I contacted Amy Garmer, then Director of the Aspen Institute's Dialogue on Public Libraries. This nationwide initiative begun in 2013 with support from the Bill & Melinda Gates Foundation's Global Libraries Program. The goal of the Dialogue, which ended in 2019, was to propose a renewed vision for public libraries in the United States. Amy provided extremely useful thoughts about the book project and general encouragement. I am indebted to Amy for introducing me to Maureen Sullivan, a chief advisor to the Dialogue who had served as President of the American Library Association (ALA), interim dean of the School of Library and Information Science at Simmons College and an instructor in library leadership at Harvard's Graduate School of Education. Maureen is now Chair of the Connecticut State Library Board.

Over the past three years Maureen served as my primary advisor as *Common Place* took shape. It turned out that one of the libraries I selected as a case study, the Otis Library in Norwich, Connecticut, is her "home" library and Maureen accompanied me on my visit there and introduced me to the director, Robert Farewell. She also made the introductions to the State Librarians in Connecticut and Vermont. Maureen read multiple drafts of *Common Place,* offered invaluable suggestions for improvement and authored the book's foreword. It is safe to say that the project could have floundered without her guidance and support. Maureen Sullivan has gained my deepest respect and appreciation and I hope the book is also something she is pleased with.

## Author

Thomas E. Johnson, Jr. was educated in design fields, receiving his MA from Harvard University, but then served twenty-five years as a U.S. Foreign Service Officer in countries around the world. Since retiring in 2012 he and his wife, Michele, have made their home in Western Massachusetts. They have two grown daughters. His previously published work appeared in journals. This is his first and last book.